the New Missionaries

Memoirs of a Foreign Adviser in Less-Developed Countries

Harvard Studies in International Development

*published jointly by the International Center for Economic Growth

Harvard Studies in International Development

the New Missionaries

Memoirs of a Foreign Adviser in Less-Developed Countries

Richard D. Mallon

HARVARD INSTITUTE FOR INTERNATIONAL DEVELOPMENT
HARVARD UNIVERSITY

DISTRIBUTED BY HARVARD UNIVERSITY PRESS

Published by the Harvard Institute for International Development

Distributed by Harvard University Press

Editing, design, and production: Sarah Newberry
Printing: Sheridan Books, Chelsea, Michigan

Library of Congress Cataloging-in-Publication Data

The new missionaries: memoirs of a foreign adviser in less
    developed countries / Richard D. Mallon
        p.   cm. — (Harvard studies in international development)
    ISBN 0-674-00348-9
    1. Developing countries—Economic policy. 2. Economic
assistance—Developing countries. 3. Developing country
specialists.   I. Harvard Institute for International Development.
II. Title. III. Series.

HC59.7.M2573   2000
338.9′009172′4—dc21
                                            00-040727
                                            CIP

Printed in the United States of America

DEDICATION ～

To Ed Mason, my mentor at the beginning of my career, and to my four grandsons,

Who represent the future.

TABLE OF CONTENTS

Principal Countries Referred to in Text

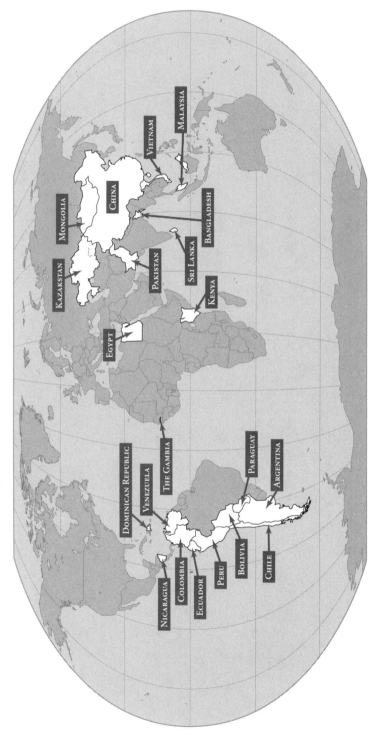

INTRODUCTION

When my wife and I and two young daughters were returning from my first two-year assignment as a foreign adviser in Pakistan in 1961, we decided to stop off in Chile, where all of my three women had been born. We thought that it would be beautiful to cross the lofty Andes mountains by train from Buenos Aires, but we had no idea what it would be like to ride the rickety Argentine railway. Our carriage was made of wood that creaked and groaned and changed shape as we jolted across the pampas. After frequent delays we finally reached the Andes in the dark of night. Then things got worse: coal smoke poured into the carriage as we chugged slowly through tunnels, forcing us to lie on the floor gasping for breath. We were horrified when our younger daughter passed out, but later she recovered with no ill effects. The only permanent damage was to our clothing, which we had to throw away at the end of our trip.

Unexpected and sometimes frightening events like this are a regular part of life in less-developed countries (LDCs). "New missionaries" – the title I shall give to policy advisers in LDCs – may not run the same risks as traditional missionaries living in jungles and other inhospitable places. On the contrary, most policy advisers today might be considered "Ugly Americans": they usually live in swank suburbs or luxury hotels (by local standards) in capital cities near the government agencies they advise. But the bureaucratic frustrations, political hazards, and xenophobia they often face can be just as threatening as physical hardships. Some say that the new missionaries lay themselves open to such threats by trying to convert local politicians and vested interests to the economic orthodoxy of free markets – they blatantly interfere in the internal affairs of foreign countries. In doing so they inevitably generate hostility from those in power who benefit from existing regulations and controls. This hostility is often evident among the bureaucrats who fear that they will lose power, but it can also drive people of modest means into the streets to protest the decontrol of food and public service prices. It is therefore not unusual for major policy reforms to be accompanied by changes in government (sometimes by violent means) and by the deportation of foreign advisers.

Policy advising did not seem like such a hazardous profession when I began my advisory career almost forty years ago. I did not consider myself to fit the dictionary definition of a missionary – one who is "strongly in favor of a program, set of principles, etc. who attempts to persuade or convert others to his position." The advisory groups I worked with were not in the policy reform business. We were mainly interested in helping to develop institutions that all modern governments require to design and implement public policy: agencies for policy planning and analysis like the U.S. Council of Economic Advisors, central banks and monetary authorities like the U.S. Federal Reserve Board, budget offices and other staff agencies and technical ministries.

Institutions of this kind in developing countries, if they existed at all, were generally ineffective and poorly staffed 40 years ago. Many governments had no way of even knowing how large their budget deficits were, much less how they contributed to monetary expansion and inflation; nor did they clearly understand the relationship among domestic policies, exchange rates, and the balance of international payments. The resulting policy contradictions and shortcomings, however, did not motivate many LDC governments to request technical assistance until foreign aid increased dramatically beginning in the 1950s. To receive this aid, LDC governments were required to prepare and justify aid-worthy projects and long-term development programs.

The dramatic increase in foreign aid for developing countries was launched in President Truman's 1949 inaugural address. Motivated by the great success of the Marshall Plan in helping to reconstruct war-ravaged Europe, he proposed the Point Four program to aid poor countries. The following year, British Commonwealth foreign ministers, meeting in Ceylon, initiated a similar program called the Colombo Plan to promote economic development in South and Southeast Asia. Other advanced countries soon joined in, and eventually the United Nations set a target for financing assistance to LDCs equal to one percent of the gross national product of donor nations. Although few donors ever complied with the target, many billions of dollars in foreign aid have since flowed yearly to developing countries, and a large share of this aid has been used to provide technical assistance.

At the outset it was not well understood how much more difficult it would be to promote institutional development in LDCs than it was to help reconstruct Europe under the Marshall Plan. Differences in levels of education and poverty, in religious and ideological beliefs, and in the strength of legal and other institutions that Americans take for granted were much greater than in the developed world. Even more problematic was the human dimension – the adviser-counterpart relationship. Policy advisers, many of whom were drawn from universities, found that their new foreign counterparts were very different from the students back home. Their new "students" were mostly mature government officials who often resented outside interference and distrusted the motives of advisers.

Affiliation with a university helped assure counterparts that foreign advisers were more interested in education than politics. But universities had problems of their own with justifying involvement in foreign advisory work. Such work was criticized for not contributing much to academic teaching and research and for not involving more members of the faculty. Universities also feared that providing advice could be interpreted as giving approval to the policies of foreign governments, even those with obnoxious reputations. This concern deepened when advisers became more embroiled in the politics of reform instead of sticking to in-service training.

The policy reform mission of foreign advisers was bolstered by changes in the purpose and flow of foreign aid and technical assistance. These changes were prompted first by international political rivalries and then mainly by major economic crises. The emphasis of technical assistance shifted from what I shall call "people-building" to helping advisees introduce policy reforms advocated by international donor agencies. Adoption of such reforms became a condition for receiving additional foreign aid. By this time I suppose it can be said that all policy advisers became new missionaries, even if they had not been earlier.

There is a distinction between old and new missionaries, however, that I always considered important. Traditional missionaries also helped develop schools, hospitals and other modern institutions in poor countries, but their primary concern was evangelical, the promulgation of the gospel that salvation can be achieved only by conversion to the faith. They were "marked by ardent or zealous enthusiasm for the cause" (dictionary definition). In other words, they were more preacher than teacher. I don't think I could ever have been a preacher – I don't have enough faith in any particular road to salvation.

The distinction between old and new missionaries in policy advising is perhaps most clearly manifested in the conflict between rapid reformers and gradualists. Advocates of rapid reform, or what is often referred to as "shock therapy," argue that a sudden turnaround in policies is necessary to rescue countries passing through an economic crisis. Gradualists like myself, on the other hand, reason that most societies need time to adjust: sudden change can create more losers than winners and therefore jeopardize the sustainability of reforms. The conflict between shock therapists and gradualists has intensified with the collapse of the Soviet bloc and rapid globalization of the world economy. Most countries are now struggling to develop internationally competitive market economies, even though many of them lack effective institutions to regulate and civilize the new rules of the game.

The intent of these memoirs, however, is not to preach. It is to let the reader make up his or her own mind on these matters. To do so, the reader will need to appreciate the challenging environment that policy advisers work in, not only professionally but personally. At the risk of appearing self-serving, I will try to develop this appreciation by drawing heavily on my own experience during the last half century, about twenty years of which have been spent in residence abroad. This journey without a destination has been sometimes dangerous and frequently frustrating, but it has never lacked the excitement of novel situations and new challenges. Hopefully, it has also succeeded in assisting poor countries to improve their capacity to solve their own problems, helping worthy counterparts to launch their professional careers, and providing my family with enough rewarding experiences to justify the sacrifices they have had to bear.

CHAPTER I ∾

PREPARATION FOR A FOREIGN ADVISORY CAREER

I grew up in Los Angeles in a family devastated by the Great Depression, with a defeated father, a strong-willed mother, and an older brother who could never cope with life's challenges. We always had enough to eat but no money for extras. My mother, a former stage actress, sold her blood and hair to finance music lessons for her boys. It was not until she began working the graveyard shift in a local aircraft factory at the beginning of World War II that we were able to move from our squalid home into a better place. It was an old Frank Lloyd Wright house where I delighted in occupying the maid's room with a separate entrance. This isolation afforded me refuge from the conflicts that raged among my mother, father, and brother and gave me great independence when I started high school. Because my parents were almost entirely preoccupied with my dysfunctional brother when they weren't working, I was in fact left pretty much on my own.

Such independence could have been disastrous for a fourteen-year-old boy, but my rearing in Christian Science made me rather boring and excruciatingly earnest. My strongest desire was to inspire trust and respect from family and friends. I was therefore selected to play Abraham Lincoln in school plays; and when I was sent to Boy's State in Sacramento, I was elected chief court justice by my peers. Later, when I was hitchhiking across the country after naval service in World War II, a man whom I had never met before even lent me his car to drive back to Los Angeles for him.

Following family tradition, I became dedicated to the arts. I attended summer art schools, became involved in the theater, and began to perform in semi-professional plays. My last performance was, however, cut short after Pearl Harbor by an air raid alert, which in effect terminated my acting career. I never returned to the stage after enlisting in the U.S. Navy upon graduation from high school. My experience as a "gob" in boot camp at San Diego was also cut short, this time by my selection for officer training. I was shipped east and after several months assigned to the NROTC at Princeton University, where I matriculated after the war with two symbolic medals and a generous veteran's scholarship.

Despite Princeton's reputation at that time as "the northernmost southern university," it was here that I developed a keen social conscience that dislodged my faith in Christian Science and dedication to the arts. I was elected president of the Cooperative Club, virtually the only eating club not reserved for Aryan gentlemen, and I linked up with a navy air pilot veteran to lead the Princeton debating team in forays throughout the East. These debating trips fulfilled not only my need for new challenges but also my love for adventure (Richard Halliburton's travel adventures were among my favorite books when I was younger). On one trip to debate Harvard, my colleague flew under the George Washington Bridge and in close circles around the Empire State Building before landing in a small athletic field adjacent to the Harvard stadium. Upon our return he was denied refueling when he stall-landed in a Connecticut airport, whereupon he ran out of gas and had to make an emergency landing in a New Jersey potato field. In addition to satisfying my youthful and sometimes rather reckless desire for adventure, these forays also stimulated my interest in the international issues that were being debated at the time.

Dick, Dad, and brother Jim, c. 1931

Mother, c. 1925

Dick and Jim with Chandler car bought for $25 during the Great Depression, c. 1939

I therefore decided to major in the School for Public and International Affairs, later renamed the Woodrow Wilson School. During the summer of 1948 I received a scholarship to do research in England for my undergraduate thesis on the organization and control of British industry, attended a Labor Party summer school in northern Wales, and hitch-hiked through France and the Low Countries to inspect postwar reconstruction. I was also interviewed as a finalist for a Rhodes Scholarship, but my main interest was in Eastern Europe and Asia. So I took a Russian language course, but I did so with flagging attention as my interest began to shift increasingly to Latin America.

In the summer of 1947 I had attended a summer camp sponsored by the Institute of World Affairs. There I met a most remarkable woman: a Chilean graduate student named Maria Ignacia Bernales Montero (Nacha for short). She first attracted my attention by helping me collect worms and sitting waist-deep in water in a leaky canoe

without complaining so as not to interrupt my fishing. When on another occasion I inadvertently closed a convertible car door on her hand and she calmly asked me to open it so she could remove her fingers, I knew that she was the right woman to accompany me on an adventurous international career.

My engagement to Nacha was, however, kept on hold after my graduation from Princeton, when I received a Woodrow Wilson fellowship to continue graduate studies. As a native Cali-

Dick the sailor, 1944

top: Engaged, 1948
right: Nacha with
    Dick at his
graduation from
    Princeton,
February 1949

fornian I was also eligible for a state veteran's scholarship, so I decided to attend the University of California at Berkeley and maintain a long-distance relationship with Nacha, who now was pursuing doctoral studies in education at Harvard. As a rather brash young man I thought that I could learn all I wanted to know about history and politics on my own, but that further formal training was necessary to understand economics. So I majored in economics at Berkeley and took one of the first courses offered by a U.S. university in the new field of Third World development.

I was happy with my studies but became increasingly dissatisfied with my long-distance international affair of the heart. Nacha agreed

Nacha, Harvard graduate student, 1948

with me, so I cut my graduate studies short in l950 and jumped on a freighter to Chile to join her back home, where "good" Latin girls were expected to get married. I was quite unprepared for what lay ahead, with only a few hundred dollars in my pocket and a few words of Spanish on my tongue.

What a ceremony! Nacha was the first of her generation in a large, distinguished, extended family to have a wedding. Gifts poured in until the room in which they were displayed overflowed – solid silver trays, crystal vases, porcelain figurines, and many practical things for starting a home. And the large Catholic church was packed with standing room only, partly I suspect to catch a glimpse of the gringo Nacha brought home. Nacha looked calm and gorgeous in her flowing white gown, never forgetting to nudge me when I was supposed to say "I do." The priest read the ceremony in English with such a Spanish intonation and accent that I didn't understand a word (it was only many years later that Nacha confessed jokingly to me that this was good grounds for annulment). After an elaborate reception, we finally drove off on our honeymoon in a car that her godfather lent us while he remained on foot in Santiago. When we returned from the honeymoon to occupy our small apartment, we found that it had been beautifully furnished by her family.

We had originally planned to stay in Chile for a year so that I could learn about Nacha's background and culture. To avoid becoming a financial burden for her family, Nacha returned to her former position at the University of Chile as a research assistant, and I got a job teaching English. But it wasn't long before I heard that the United Nations Economic Commission for Latin America (ECLA) was hiring a junior economist in its Santiago headquarters. I applied for the position and was hired as a member of the local staff. Little did I realize at the time that this was the beginning of a seven-year stint at ECLA.

It was a fascinating place to work, especially for the only young gringo on the staff. Raul Prebisch, founder of the Argentine central bank and well-known international economist, had just been named executive secretary of ECLA the year before. He had assembled an impressive group of Latin American professionals, many of whom were refugees from dictatorships back home and represented a wide spectrum of ideologies. The environment was electrifying – a sense of new discovery pervaded the offices and corridors, where animated discussions took place almost daily with a sense of mission unique in the developing world. My colleagues were intent on mapping out a strategy for development of the region that was not dependent on the great industrial powers, most of which behaved in a dog-eat-dog manner during the inter-war years and were still struggling to recover from Second World War devastation. They believed that Latin American countries could lift themselves up by their own bootstraps by creating new industrial societies that provided high-paying jobs to peasants trapped in semi-feudal agriculture and by raising labor productivity through the introduction of modern technology.

The main idea espoused by Prebisch and ECLA was that poor countries on the periphery of the world economy were relegated to providing food and raw materials to the rest of the world in an unequal

Wedding, August 12, 1950

6

exchange that favored exporters of manufactures. Peripheral countries could not compete with already developed manufacturing centers, however, unless they adopted concerted strategies aimed at creating industrial complexes that would produce for protected regional markets that enabled the peripheral countries to achieve economies of scale. It was therefore the mission of ECLA to help member countries prepare national development studies and plans to identify such strategies. The nationalistic, even isolationist, tone of ECLA's mission generated considerable political controversy with international organizations such as the World Bank, as well as with the United States and other governments. Partly for this reason, ECLA's strategy was at least partially disavowed in later years, especially after the catastrophic international debt crisis began in 1982. In the 1950s, however, it provided an education for me that could not be found in any U.S. university.

Some six months after joining ECLA I had learned enough Spanish to participate actively in what was going on. I was elected vice-president of the labor union of local staff, which was headed by a brilliant young Chilean economist, Pedro Vuskovic, a marxist who later became a key minister in the cabinet of President Salvador Allende. We had many adversarial discussions on economic issues, but the only success I remember having in changing his mind was to convince him that, contrary to local macho custom, he should open a joint bank account in his wife's name so that she could draw funds when he was away on ECLA missions abroad. I soon began to travel on ECLA missions abroad myself – across the high Andean plateau to drink *chicha* in Indian villages, to the Bolivian jungle in a jeep, across Lake Titicaca in a wood-burning steamer, up Macchu Picchu to pick wild strawberries among the ruins, into the old Spanish fortifications of Cartagena, even to Rio for a week to celebrate the Carnival with Brazilian friends. On these trips my colleagues, several of whom would later occupy important posts in their governments back home, did their best to turn me into a "gringo de agua dulce" (taken from the Chilean expression "fresh water sailor," meaning one who knows how to sail but is not really an "old salt").

I was regularly promoted until I became a member of the international staff of ECLA, with a dollar salary and duty-free import privileges that allowed us to reciprocate the generous support Nacha's family gave us. Until our daughters began to arrive, we almost always ate dinner at Nacha's parents' home with her sisters, her brother, and frequent guests – a very animated affair beginning at 9:30 P.M. that tested my endurance to understand several conversations in Spanish going on at the same time. On weekends a visit to the cavernous old aunts' house downtown to participate in larger extended-family gatherings was a 'must'. And for vacations we often went to San Pancho, the sprawling family farm located a couple of hundred miles south of Santiago near the coast. Even after our daughters arrived, we would pack them in our old '35 Ford, with a baby bath tub, kerosene heaters, and other paraphernalia strapped to the running boards, and take off for the country place, bouncing over dirt roads and fording streams along the way. When Nacha was pregnant, a cousin flew her there in a rented plane.

Complete immersion in Chilean family life (there was no time or real interest to associate with the local foreign community) taught me many lessons about Latin ways of thinking and behaving. At first I had refused to visit San Pancho because I disapproved of *inquilinismo*, a form of indentured servitude then prevalent on Chilean farms. But Nacha convinced me that my attitude was intolerant: one can follow one's own conscience at home, but a guest must respect the customs of his host. I learned the subtle distinction between intimate and formal terms of address: the choice between *tu* and *usted* often reflects differences in social status as well as age and friendship, and use of the wrong pronoun can confuse or offend someone very deeply. Socially acceptable communication is also more indirect than gringos are accustomed to: one never brings up a serious topic, even in non-social conversation, without first trying to bond with the person by asking about family or other unrelated matters. On the other hand, cultured Latins have a keen sense of ridicule, especially for naive behavior: there is no country in Latin America where fun is not made of certain foreigners (especially those who try to "go native") or of unsophisticated country bumpkins.

It was only natural for us to bring up our two daughters like Chilean children. As babies they were trussed up like little papooses in tight wrappings and had nannies to help take care of them. We also gave them both Spanish and English names. The first-born was named Florencia (after my father-in-law Florencio Bernales) Elizabeth (after my mother), which contracted into the handy nickname Florel. We named our second daughter Ignacia (the proper name for Nacha) Irene (because we liked it), but we called her Nanine, another kind of contraction.

Nacha, Florel, Nanine, and Dick, 1956

Health conditions in Chile at this time were not as good as in the U.S., but only Florel contracted scarlet fever and neither daughter suffered from widespread typhoid (to which only Nacha fell prey). We also selected a local physician to perform serious surgery on Nanine's hips. Both of the girls started talking only Spanish to everyone including Nacha and me, so we did not suspect that they were learning English by overhearing conversations between us. We only realized how much they were actually learning when Florel started translating our confidences to the maids, to our great embarrassment.

These were professionally rewarding and mostly happy times for the family, but in 1957 Nacha and I decided that it was finally time for me to return to the U.S. to complete my PhD. I was perplexed by questions about public policy and economic development that I did not feel I could answer without further formal education. I was convinced that the person who could most help me answer these questions was Prof. Simon Kuznets, later a Nobel Prize laureate. He was currently teaching at Johns Hopkins University, so I applied and received a good scholarship offer, only to hear shortly thereafter that Kuznets would soon be moving to Harvard. I then applied to Harvard, was offered a generous scholarship, and accepted it despite the fact that Harvard did not provide a professional position for Nacha as another university had.

This was to be Nacha's role for the rest of our lives: accommodating to the priorities of my work while postponing her own. She could have been a force in advancing education in Chile, but instead she chose to play the seldom appreciated role of accompanying spouse of a career foreign adviser. This role included dismantling our homes when we moved from one place to another. So when we decided that I should depart first to set things up in Boston, she was left with the chore of organizing her later trip with the kids and a maid, selling our new car for a good price (important for financing our living expenses at Harvard), and even fending off

Florel and Nanine, 1958: proper Bostonian little ladies

seasickness to take care of her charges while sailing to the U.S. through the Caribbean in the tail of a major hurricane.

Nacha and entourage arrived in Boston on October l, 1957, to move into an old house I'd bought and furnished with the essentials. This was a completely new experience for all of us. Our daughters were frustrated by their limited English, although they learned incredibly fast – six-year-old Florel was even chosen to be master of ceremonies at her school's celebration that Christmas! And our Chilean maid, whom we brought with us so that Nacha would not be tied down in the house and could earn a little extra money to supplement my scholarship, learned that a bright sunny day in winter was not warm enough to go outdoors without a coat, and that laundry hung on the line would freeze solid as a board. And I quickly found out that the driveway had to be shoveled after every snowfall so that it would not later turn to ice.

Meanwhile, at Harvard I selected economic development as my major field of study and soon met Prof. Ed Mason, dean of what later became the John F. Kennedy School of Government. (Professor Kuznets did not come to Harvard until the fall of 1958.) Mason was a prominent figure in the development field and already headed a small technical assistance program. Part of the program consisted of the Public Service Fellows in Economic Development, a group of mid-career public servants from Third World countries who came to Harvard for a year to update their knowledge and "recharge their batteries." The largest component of the program was a pair of advisory projects on national planning in Pakistan and Iran.

Before the end of my first year of study I was appointed assistant to the Public Service Fellows, and half way into my second year I was offered the position of general economic adviser to the Pakistan Planning Commission in Karachi. The timing was awkward – our family had only barely settled into a new home, and ironically I hadn't yet had time to take any course with Prof. Kuznets. But a two-year resident advisory position in Pakistan offered me an opportunity to acquire practical professional knowledge in a totally different environment from the one I was acquainted with in Latin America.

Pakistan was a poor Muslim country that had only recently achieved independence. Although English was the official working language, the populace preferred to speak in a number of local dialects. Integrating into such an alien culture would be a most difficult task. The most daunting prospect from a family point of view was the real danger of infection from a variety of exotic diseases including malaria and cholera. (On the other hand, we had faced similar dangers in Chile, and the U.S. was experiencing the polio scare at this time). So Nacha and I decided, with some trepidation, that this was a worthwhile opportunity to advance my career, even though we had not yet considered the possibility of my becoming a professional foreign adviser.

CHAPTER II ⁓

INITIATION OF A FOREIGN ADVISORY CAREER

Nacha and I, our two young daughters, and our Chilean maid took off for Pakistan in the spring of 1959, passing through Hawaii where we were booked on an inaugural turbo prop flight to Tokyo. The flight had not been cleared by the FAA before departure, so we flew free of charge – a nice piece of Mallon luck to begin our new adventure! Our poor daughters were walking zombies by the time we arrived in Tokyo and were met by a barrage of lights and cameras, but the most traumatic experience was the sense of being completely alien. Japanese women, the older ones still dressed in kimonos, would stop in the street to observe and touch our daughters' golden hair. We continued the next day on one of the first Comet jet aircraft flights to Hong Kong for shopping and then on to Calcutta, where a blast of hundred-degree heat discouraged us from getting off to stretch our legs (we would soon get used to it). When we finally reached Karachi we were welcomed at the airport by most of the Harvard project personnel.

We were taken directly to pre-assigned living quarters (the only time this ever happened to us when taking up residence in a new country). Our house was a sprawling, single-story building in a walled compound with that of another project family who had also brought a nanny with them to help take care of their two little daughters. Bringing a nanny was reassuring because all of the house staff was male in this Muslim society. The staff we inherited consisted of a "bearer" or chief butler and a Christian "sweeper" to do his dirty work (a question of social status and religion, because no self-respecting Muslim could clean toilets); a cook who insisted on having a *hamal* (dish washer) to maintain his own status; a *chokidar* (night watchman); and three part-time servants – a *dhobi* (laundryman), a *mali* (gardener), and a *dhersi* (tailor) to repair and make clothing and linens. With this formidable household staff one might think we were able to live in the lap of idle luxury – far from it!

On the beach with friends in Pakistan, 1959

The "mem-sahib" or lady of the house was expected to behave like the CEO of a small enterprise, handing out daily assignments, controlling purchases and the allotment of supplies from the "go-down" (a locked room where all the goodies were kept), supervising performance, protecting against theft, adjudicating disputes among the staff, and getting involved in their personal problems (usually financial). The *dhersi*, for example, needed a year's advance in wages to finance a dowry and wedding ceremony for his daughter! This situation did not last long, however. The first crisis was triggered by the bearer, who had been trained in the British colonial tradition as a personal valet of the sahib. After Nacha found him massaging my toes one evening instead of cleaning her shoes as she had ordered, he was soon looking for another job. By the time we left Pakistan the permanent house staff consisted only of a *hamal*.

The house not only was well populated but also sheltered little lizards clinging to the walls and ceilings. At first we tried to get rid of the uninvited visitors, fearing they could join us in bed. But we soon found out that these geckos were helpful in ridding the house of mosquitoes and other insects and even in warning us of the invasion of snakes. So we let them multiply freely and never found any snakes in the house, although this may have been due to Nacha's taking the added precaution of plugging the drains in the bathroom and kitchen every night. We also learned other useful things, such as turning off the hot-water heater in summer so that it could store cool water (unheated water was stored in a roof tank and became scalding by midday). And we even learned to sleep soundly in spite of the loud braying of donkeys all night. The only thing we could do nothing about was repair the damage to a shipment of personal effects that was off-loaded by mistake in Bombay, where it spent the monsoon in the open and was finally delivered full of dead rats and ruined family photos.

While Nacha was coming to grips with her little enterprise, I started work in the Planning Commission. The first impression was depressing. The Commission occupied a run-down building with walls stained by the spittle of betel-nut chewers and with the odor of toilets wafting down the hallways, which were cluttered with ragged looking "peons" who didn't seem to have much to do but chat and play with their bare toes. They formed the lower rank (just above the sweepers) of a pecking order in which one's status was symbolized by the number of people one could order around. I quickly learned not to by-pass this pecking order by trying to do things for myself; if an underling felt ignored, he could seek revenge by misplacing something like an urgently needed file. (All documents were kept in bundles bound in red tape, a British colonial legacy from which the term for excessive bureaucratic procedure originated.) Verb conjugations in Urdu actually distinguish between asking directly or asking someone to ask someone to do something. Ringing for a peon did have at least one advantage: one could stay seated under a ceiling fan to dry one's sweat-soaked clothes.

Nacha and girls at seashell market in Karachi, 1960

Relationships between members of the senior staff were also governed by a pecking order. At the top of this order were members of the Pakistani Civil Service,

Poverty in Bengal

an elite cadre of paternalistic general administrators ranked according to seniority. The PC chairman, formerly head of the national police, was a member of this cadre. He ruled like an monarch, passing down decisions that were not open to debate. The deputy chairman was a nice old gentleman preparing for retirement from the civil service who deferred to the chairman. And the chief economist, who did not belong to the elite cadre and was not well-trained in economics, was content to pass on orders received from above. This was certainly not a collegial environment conducive to professional discussion of development programs and policies. It was more like what one might expect in the central planning bureau of the Soviet Union.

The Planning Commission was not, however, a Soviet-style planning agency; it was more like a combination of the U.S. Council of Economic Advisers and Budget Bureau, except that it dealt primarily with capital expenditures. The PC was the top-level staff body responsible for screening government investment projects, assigning priorities, formulating the annual investment program, and budgeting its financing, especially from abroad. Foreign aid and loans were of critical importance because they financed about half the investment program. I suspect that this was the main reason the government wanted foreign advisers – to help document requests for foreign assistance. Participation of Harvard advisers in preparing these docu-

Beauty in Kashmir

ments strengthened their international credibility. Aside from this, I did not feel that we were doing very much to strengthen the institution, which was ostensibly the main purpose of the project. We did not conduct any formal in-house training, and we never became involved in the really challenging aspects of the Commission's work: helping to examine alternative development strategies and to analyze major policy trade-offs.

When the project began, five years earlier, the Harvard advisory group apparently did play a key role in getting the PC started, defining its mission, and "weaving the planning idea into the mind and method of the policy-making and executive branches of government" (quotation from an evaluation report by the Ford Foundation). But nothing like this occurred during my tour of duty. Advisers were almost exclusively engaged in helping to prepare Pakistan's Second Five-Year Plan. Preparation of the plan raised some important strategic and policy issues: how to improve conditions in the impoverished province of East Pakistan; how to fit the mammoth Indus River basin works (dividing irrigation waters between Pakistan and India) into the development program; and what to do about the 1960 population census figures that contradicted plan projections. Decisions on these and other major questions were not subjected to careful professional analysis and discussion but made by administrative fiat. I

17

remember in particular the an-
ger of the two Harvard advisers
stationed in Dhaka who flew all
the way to Karachi to make a
case for East Pakistan but were
summarily turned away by the
chairman.

Working relations between
the eight Harvard advisers stationed in Karachi and their local
counterparts were more collegial
at the technical level. I was assigned two counterparts. The
first was the deputy chief economist, a junior member of the
Civil Service who had married
into the family of a top government official. I almost never

Bengali boatman

saw him because he was busy representing the PC in interministerial
meetings on subjects I was never consulted about. My other counterpart was a charming and thoughtful East Pakistani who headed the
long-term planning division. We did some interesting work together,
but I think I was the one who learned most from our association. He
became a personal friend who instructed me in Pakistani culture and
music, and I helped teach his little son to play chess when invited to
his home. This kind of friendship between Pakistani and foreign families was quite unusual because of multiple cultural barriers.

One barrier was of course language. Nacha and I tried hard to learn
Urdu from a teacher we hired shortly after arriving in Pakistan. I mas-
tered enough to communicate with guest house servants when I traveled outside of Karachi, but it was not very useful otherwise. The local elite preferred to speak English or, in especially cultured gatherings, to talk to each other in Persian. Most other people preferred to
speak in one of several local languages, especially if they thought we
understood Urdu and were therefore trying to "trespass" on their turf.
We discovered that language is almost as important as religion or caste
in defining one's identity in the subcontinent, as was later illustrated
in East Pakistan: the attempt to make Urdu the official language in
place of Bengali was one of the main causes for the break-up of the
country and the creation of Bangladesh.

Armed guard assigned to "protect" me during trip in Baluchistan, Pakistan

Other barriers were equally difficult for foreigners like us to cross. Most of our counterparts simply could not afford to reciprocate invitations because their incomes were so much lower than ours. Or if they lived in typical extended family compounds, older relatives were likely to be orthodox Muslims who felt obliged to destroy dinnerware contaminated by infidels. Perhaps the most insuperable barrier, however, was the status of women. Even the wives of our professional counterparts were usually much less educated and sophisticated than their husbands: they spoke no English, did not know how to use a knife and fork, and in social gatherings would sit silently in a circle in the women's sector often playing with their toes (what is it about toes in Pakistan!). Our few Pakistani family friends therefore belonged to the westernized elite, who often seemed to feel in limbo between two alien cultures, much as we did.

Nacha and I became increasingly aware of this cultural tension after Nacha was appointed high-school principal at the Karachi American School. Most students belonged to the official American community that lived in an isolated enclave, socializing almost exclusively with each other and purchasing their needs in the U.S. commissary. We did not have access to the commissary, so our daughters were awed when their schoolmates bragged about what they could get there. So much so that when I took Nanine to see the sparkling lights and deco-

Downtown traffic in Dhaka

rations at the senior prom that Nacha arranged, she pulled on my sleeve and asked reverently, "Is this the commissary?"

The feeling of longing for (and perhaps glorifying) the unattainable was much more poignant in the case of young Pakistanis. One lovely Pakistani teacher at the American School longed to emulate the western way of life, but she was obliged to go into purdah when she visited her native village and was under intense pressure to accept an arranged marriage. A young colleague of mine at the Planning Commission found this kind of pressure so unbearable that he had to seek psychiatric help.

I began to wonder whether we Harvard advisers, rather than helping to strengthen indigenous capacity for policy planning and analysis, were only stirring up discontent among our young counterparts. What contribution were we making by trying to teach them to analyze and challenge received wisdom in a traditional society in which all important decisions were passed down from above? I became even more dubious when I was appointed acting director of the project and observed what was happening with other advisers, both in Karachi and in the provincial capitals. They were just as distant as I personally felt from understanding and actively participating in the process of policy planning and analysis. It seemed quite clear that we were being used mainly as window dressing to justify requests for more foreign aid.

By the end of 1960 a new, permanent project director named Richard Gilbert arrived to take over. He was an exceptional man driven by a desire to make a difference. After spending days with me and other advisers arguing about alternative strategies, he launched an active campaign to enhance the relevance of the advisory group. He identified a promising rural development project in East Pakistan directed by a charismatic leader and persuaded the USAID director to support expansion of the project into a massive rural public works program. Once the program was successfully underway, he then went outside the Planning Commission to establish close personal ties with the very talented finance minister, who began to rely on him for advice. In this way he broke out of the authoritarian straitjacket in which the advisory group had been trapped, and helped the Planning Commission assume a staff role to the central government on virtually all economic policy issues. Although these events unfolded after my tour of duty ended in the spring of 1961, I kept in touch and was deeply impressed by what Gilbert was able to accomplish, although his high-profile political posture disturbed me. This posture also contributed to the demise of the project when a new Pakistani administration came to power.

Then another thought crossed my mind: would Gilbert have been able to accomplish so much if he had no competent counterpart staff to work with? He did very little himself to train junior counterparts in the Planning Commission, but he benefited from the intensive in-service training provided by previous Harvard advisers. I was so impressed by the team of young counterparts we worked with that before I left I invited them to tea at the Metropole Hotel in Karachi to express my appreciation. Some of them stayed in contact with me and later occupied prominent positions in their government and in international organizations such as the World Bank; one of them, Mahbub-ul-Haq, even became finance minister of Pakistan.

We departed from Pakistan with mixed feelings. My work and our efforts to integrate into Pakistani society had been frustrating, but our family had risen to the challenge: our daughters thrived on buffalo milk and remained healthy despite a few scares from attacks of diarrhea, bluebottle jelly fish, and threats from roving packs of pariah dogs; Nacha survived the mosquitoes and complications from a miscarriage; and I managed to keep afloat when carried away by the

Snow again! Returning from Pakistan through Europe, 1961

undertow in the turbulent monsoon surf near our beach hut. We felt a little insecure when I once contacted the local police and was told that they would be delighted to come help us if we sent a car, because they did not have transportation. But nothing serious ever happened to us.

Closing up the house was quite a chore, especially when an army of packers came to box our personal effects including the cat, which we rescued just in time after hearing its desperate screech. We took advantage of our trip home to tour through southern Europe. What a pleasure to eat familiar food and to see snow again! Our daughters were a little young to fully appreciate ancient monuments, cathedrals and art galleries – at one point Nanine stood in front of a Greek temple, lifted her arms, and cried disapprovingly, "Marble, marble, marble, everything marble! Please show me something new." But in general we all had a good time driving up through Italy into the Alps, across to Paris, through the Loire and down to Spain, eating outdoor picnics in scenic places along the way.

We caught a boat in Barcelona and spent a couple of weeks crossing the Atlantic to Buenos Aires, where we boarded a train so that we could enjoy seeing the Andes as we crossed over to Chile. What a disaster! The wooden carriages must have been of pre–World War I vintage – they rattled and rocked so violently that windows wouldn't stay closed and doors changed shape. When the kids said they would prefer to use the upper bunks, the porter warned that it would be dangerous – they could be thrown out while sleeping. The train was so far behind schedule that we could see nothing as we crossed the Andes at night; and then we were nearly asphyxiated with coal smoke from the locomotive while passing through tunnels.

After a short visit in Santiago, we decided that I should return to Cambridge alone to find a place to live and start preparing my doctoral dissertation. On the way I stopped in the Brazilian northeast to visit a former ECLA colleague who was directing a very innovative land reform and development program there. Was this the kind of work that I would find most rewarding, or should I become a professional foreign adviser, a profession that I considered to be an educational one without direct decision-making power? And then there was the third option of following an academic career. These were some of the thoughts passing through my mind as I returned to Harvard.

CHAPTER III ⌒
THE HARVARD DEVELOPMENT ADVISORY SERVICE

*M*y priority upon returning to Harvard in 1961 was to prepare a PhD dissertation so that I could receive the magic
letters and get on with my career. I chose as my topic
Pakistan development planning. Fortunately, my thesis committee
consisted of Professor Mason and two former project directors who
had returned to Harvard. Although my dissertation was not a distinguished piece of work, I was able to finish it quickly and, not unex-
pectedly, have it approved easily by a sympathetic committee.

I also wanted to move my family back to the United States in time
for our daughters to enter the spring term at school. They were enrolled in a Chilean school at the time, which was good for brushing
up their Spanish, but we did not want them to get too far behind in
the U.S. curriculum. So I became a short-term USAID consultant to
Chile to earn my passage and a little extra money, which came in very
handy during this lean period. I helped Nacha pack up and ship our
things and fly back to Boston in February 1962, awkwardly with me
in first class and my three women in economy.

We moved temporarily into the cramped apartment I had rented
in Somerville while we puzzled over where to buy a house. We decided to return to the same neighborhood in Newton where we had
lived two years earlier, so that our daughters could see old friends and
familiar surroundings again. They had already lived in five different
houses in three countries. Providing some continuity in their vaga-
bond lives seemed especially desirable after I decided to join the newly
formed Harvard Development Advisory Service, which obligated me
to spend about half my time overseas.

The Development Advisory Service (DAS) was a unique concept.
It was established in 1962 with Ford Foundation support as a regular
part of Harvard University to provide a stable institutional base for a
small permanent corps of economists, who would divide their time
more or less equally between residence abroad and at Harvard. While
abroad they would lead DAS projects in developing countries; back

at Harvard they would use their overseas experience to enrich research and teaching on third world development at the university. For me the DAS appeared to offer an ideal career, especially in comparison with the purely academic position I had interviewed for at another university. The DAS position would combine my interest in helping poor countries with the opportunity to recharge my batteries periodically in an intellectually stimulating environment. But like all good things, there were problems too that I did not fully appreciate when I joined the DAS as a tenured fellow.

A major problem that would surface periodically during my career at Harvard was the conflict between two different cultures, similar to the conflicts that occur when firms in different lines of business decide to merge. A university like Harvard is in the business of pushing back the frontier of knowledge through cutting-edge research and of educating an elite to become professors in the best universities and future leaders in public and private life. Few top scholars in the field of economics are interested in the type of work that foreign advisers usually do. As academics they are under pressure to *generalize* from empirical experience. They advance their careers by formulating and testing new hypotheses and theories, by publishing their findings in leading professional journals, and by receiving personal recognition for their authorship.

The DAS, on the other hand, was in the business of helping poor countries to solve practical problems of development and of training competent technocrats. Foreign advisers are more concerned with *particularizing* than with generalizing from empirical experience. Their job is to identify policy problems and to help craft solutions in specific country situations. Expressions like "do not quote without permission of the author" don't appear on their field studies and papers; they are happy to be plagiarized by local counterparts. Indeed, it seemed to me that the ideal method of work was to carry out policy studies jointly with counterparts without pride of authorship.

This culture clash later contributed to the uneasiness, and sometimes the downright hostility, that some scholars and students felt toward the DAS. They were especially uneasy about the responsibility Harvard implicitly assumed for DAS policy advice to foreign countries, especially to those with distasteful governments. This is an issue that inevitably polarizes opinion, as it does today in the dispute over official U.S. policy toward repressive foreign governments. Some people sincerely think that "engagement" with such governments is the most effective way to bring about change, whereas others believe that working with them is immoral. I personally believe that this is a practical issue, not a moral one. If government restrictions on open discussion, access to information, and personnel selection are onerous enough to impede professional collaboration, then technical assistance would probably be ineffective anyway. Otherwise, the chances are that exposure of counterparts to competitive market analysis and public policy debates will over time help loosen up restrictions (or get advisers thrown out of the country).

The culture clash in the university also raised a fundamental academic question that was never to be resolved satisfactorily: could DAS advisers who spent most of their time working on mundane development problems abroad meet Harvard's rigorous teaching and research standards? The prospect of DAS advisers being considered second-class citizens at Harvard did not put me off so much as the difficulty I foresaw of collaborating with academic scholars bent on promoting and defending their reputations in competition with prominent peers. On the one hand, I was afraid that when they served as consultants with DAS projects overseas they would behave like traditional missionaries, intent on spreading the faith instead of helping to train local counterparts to sort through policy options. On the other, I was worried that when back at Harvard they would be more interested in using the data that DAS advisers gathered for their own purposes instead of collaborating as colleagues in joint research.

The potential incompatibility between scholar and adviser reminded me many years later of the controversy between performer and teacher that embroiled the Annenberg Foundation grant to the Artsvision program for New York City public schools. The grant was made largely to finance periodic visits by outside performers instead of regular classroom instruction by professional arts teachers, despite the objection that virtuoso performers were not necessarily good teachers. Renowned dancers, like distinguished scholars, might impress audiences with their brilliance, but they were not often as good as professional teachers at helping students learn the steps.

It fortunately turned out that my misgivings were exaggerated. A number of distinguished scholars at Harvard (such as Nobel prize winner Simon Kuznets) were also good at "teaching the steps" to DAS project counterparts. They were not available for long-term assignments overseas, but short visits could be very effective if resident advisers were present to follow up the work they started. The key to capacity building for short-term consultants was basically the same as for resident advisers: roll up your sleeves and work side by side with local colleagues. For this kind of collaboration to work, it was essential to create a climate for free and open discussion without posturing rank or reputation. Such a climate is not easy to create: it did not exist among our senior counterparts during my time in Pakistan, nor did it in another DAS project with a government research institute in Greece.

Our chief adviser at the Greek institute was frustrated by the reluctance of local counterparts to submit their papers for peer review, so when one of them finally brought a paper to him for criticism he was overjoyed. The paper was not very good, but he spent a great deal of time preparing what he considered constructive comments. Soon afterward another counterpart appeared at his office shouting, "You tore my paper apart for my worst enemy, who's now using your criticism to destroy my reputation in the institute."

Getting sucked into local personality squabbles and power struggles was an occupational hazard that I was familiar with from my previous work in Latin America and Pakistan. A foreign adviser is usually under suspicion from the start, sometimes because of xenophobia but more often because counterparts fear that he will compete unequally with them for power and influence, taking sides in local rivalries. This fear is understandable. The counterpart system emerged in colonial Africa with the speed-up of Africanization programs directed by expatriates who sometimes acted as if they were carrying the torch of reason to natives who lived in darkness. Local counterparts served mostly as apprentices in subservient working relationships, not as colleagues. And few if any local staff in developing countries ever had a professor with whom they could establish a collegial relationship. Professors sermonized from a high podium and, at least in former British colonies, expected students to leap to their feet when they entered the classroom.

I believed that a foreign adviser had as much to learn from local counterparts as they could learn from the adviser. He or she was expected to have more know-how in the art of national planning and policy analysis, whereas they should know a great deal more about local socioeconomic conditions and political constraints. Both kinds of knowledge were equally important at the macro policy level at which I worked. At this level the main responsibility of government is to try to reconcile competing claims on limited national resources, a balancing act that requires a good sense of which way gravity is pulling.

As an idealistic young professional who considered it unethical for foreigners to intervene in internal affairs of another country, I was determined to steer clear of local rivalries for power and influence. I would be a two-handed economist – "on the one hand this, but on the other that" – without insisting on my own policy opinions. I didn't think this even-handed approach would diminish my effectiveness as an adviser, because the *techniques* of economic analysis are politically neutral in market economies. It is the choice among alternative policy *actions* that is fundamentally a political decision.

Populist politicians, for example, may advocate greater government spending on attractive social programs; but economic analysis makes clear that unless government has the will and the power to redistribute real income from rich to poor to pay for such programs, the inevitable result is accelerated inflation and deeper poverty in the long run. The choice and timing of measures to reduce inflation or balance a government's budget, on the other hand, are political decisions. Some advocates of rapid, drastic reforms speak as if "shock therapy" were grounded on solid economic principles, that "chopping off a cat's tail all at once is less painful than doing it bit by bit." But people are not like cats, which have no choice in the matter. If the pain of shock therapy is severe and long-lasting, people are inclined to rise up against their masters unless they are forcefully repressed or are convinced that previous policies were even worse.

Maintaining political neutrality as an economic adviser nevertheless turned out to be much more difficult in practice than I anticipated, as we shall see in subsequent chapters. The difficulty was created in part by the increasing insistence of project funders on providing technical assistance to implement specific policy reforms. But I also discovered that the roles of foreign adviser as colleague and authority figure actually tend to reinforce each other. Advisers without any power or influence are less likely to be taken seriously or may even be ignored. They are therefore obliged, at least to some extent, to become involved in local power relations if they want to be effective.

Does this mean that I consider my successor in Pakistan, Richard Gilbert, a model new missionary? No, he was not a missionary but a "conquistador," the most charismatic and persuasive colleague I worked with since Raul Prebisch. Gilbert was a high profile activist, competing openly for power and influence in the Pakistani political arena. I still don't think this is the proper role for a foreign adviser hired to strengthen local institutions and train counterparts in policy planning and analysis.

My first assignment as a DAS cadre member was, however, reassuring with regard to most of my concerns. Prof. Mason asked me to organize a couple of projects in Latin America, where I felt confident I understood the language and culture. The projects were intended to strengthen the capacity of national planning agencies in Argentina and Colombia under the Alliance for

Nanine and Florel before departure to Argentina, 1963

Progress program. This was a subject I was quite familiar with in countries where I had worked while at ECLA. Furthermore, the projects were to be funded by the Ford Foundation and the Inter-American Development Bank, both of which were interested mainly in training and institution building, not in pressuring governments to adopt specific reforms. So I set out in the summer of 1962 to talk to the director of the Alliance for Progress, to learn more about the proposed projects, to contact knowledgeable people, and to negotiate with government officials.

Agreements were eventually reached to undertake both projects, although the political situation in Argentina remained uncertain. The military regime had agreed to hold elections to choose a new civilian government, but it was of course impossible to know in advance what the new government would be like and whether it would really be interested in receiving technical assistance from the DAS. We decided to go ahead nevertheless, so the admiral in charge of national planning arranged for an elaborate contract-signing ceremony aboard a naval vessel. Prof. Mason flew down to Buenos Aires to represent Harvard in the ceremony, which gave us a premonition of

left: Mallon family drives through redwood tree in Yosemite National Park, 1963. below: Déjà vu! Brother Jim and Dick at same tree, c. 1941.

what was to come. The ship wouldn't start, so the contract was signed by a red-faced admiral with the boat still tied to the dock.

Under the circumstances we thought it wise to diversify our risks by starting a second project with a private economic research institute in Buenos Aires. If the government project didn't work out, we could shift our resources to the private one. Furthermore, the two projects could become complementary if the national planning agency was willing to contract some research out to the institute. This kind of public-private sector collaboration was unusual in Latin America, but I thought it could be beneficial for both parties.

So Nacha and I started to pack up our things and move again, this time to Argentina. I thought that the project in Colombia was not as complicated as the one in Argentina and could more easily be handled by someone who did not participate in setting it up. We wanted to give the newly elected Argentine government time to organize itself before arriving, so we took off on a leisurely trip by car across the United States as soon as our daughters finished their school term. We thought that it would be a good idea for them to see something of their own country before going overseas, and we wanted my parents in Los Angeles to see their grandchildren again before they returned from abroad as teenagers.

CHAPTER IV 〜
RESIDENCE IN ARGENTINA

*A*fter stopping in Chile for a brief visit, our family continued together to Buenos Aires (this time by air!), where we arrived in the spring of 1963. In the southern hemisphere, this time of year is of course the fall, so the timing was right for our daughters to begin the new term at the American School. The timing was quite wrong, however, to try to start an advisory project with the National Development Council (CONADE).

The caretaker military regime was still in the process of handing over power to a newly elected civilian government with which we had no previous contact. The admiral-director with whom we arranged the project had departed, and CONADE was left in the hands of a civilian administrator who had no inkling of what was going to happen next. Worse, he was unwilling to take any initiative to try to find out. So I was left in limbo with my family, unable to start work, establish residence, or clear our shipment of household effects through customs.

Not wishing to remain in a hotel for an indefinite period, we decided to move into a housekeeping apartment deceptively named Sweet Home. The greatest inconvenience of the place was that it was located near downtown Buenos Aires, a full hour by bus from the American School. The girls took their long commute in good spirit, though, and Nacha kept busy buying the things we needed until we could get our hands on our household effects. Meanwhile, I was able to get our other project started with the DiTella Economic Research Center, but my main concern remained how to make contact with the new government. I decided with some trepidation to go right to the top.

President-elect Illia was a physician from the provincial city of Cordoba, from which he arrived in Buenos Aires about the same time I did to organize his new administration. I located his hotel and left my card with a request for an interview, expecting at best that one of his assistants would ask me to wait patiently until the new head of

CONADE was appointed. To my dismay I received a message a couple of days later saying that the president would see me the following morning. When I entered his hotel I was caught up in a mob of job seekers and hangers-on in a large, smoke-filled anteroom. I announced myself and lit my pipe to add to the haze as I waited. While curiously observing the feverish activity, I suddenly noticed a tall, white-haired figure approaching me from a side room. Before I had time to take the pipe out of my mouth, he grabbed both of my jacket lapels, pinning my arms down. So the first words I exchanged with the new president were spoken with clenched teeth, trying to hang on to my pipe while not blowing smoke in his face.

We agreed to see each other the next morning when the president said he would have more time to talk. And talk we did the following day, not only with the president but with his whole economic team. Dr. Illia was very gracious and promised to implement our technical assistance project, but I could see that his economic team was very skeptical. They were popular nationalists who previously had occupied important positions in the regime that took power after the overthrow of Juan Peron a decade earlier. It was quite understandable for them to wonder what a gringo could do to help them, especially one whom they had never met before and who had negotiated a deal with the departing military authorities.

Nothing happened thereafter until I accidentally bumped into the economic team again in the lobby of a downtown hotel several days later. They were accompanied by Raul Prebisch, my former boss in ECLA who had taken leave in 1955 to become their chief economic adviser and had now returned briefly for consultation. He greeted me warmly and reintroduced me to the economic team, saying that I was a very special gringo who knew a lot about Latin America. From that moment on I became a kind of stand-in for Prebisch as their new economic adviser. Mallon luck struck again, but as we shall see it turned out to be a mixed blessing.

The first assignment I was given, even before inauguration of the president, was to prepare a short-term recovery program to lift the economy out of recession. This work provided an excellent opportunity for me to involve the staff of CONADE and to get to know them better. The civilian administrator was delighted to be "in the loop" and gave me a spacious office adjoining his own with carte blanche to hand out assignments to the idle staff. I felt a little uncomfortable usurping this kind of authority, but the newly appointed head of CONADE,

Dick with President Illia and the secretary of commerce of Argentina, 1964

Roque Carranza, was not yet available to take over. He was still in Chile finishing his job with an organization affiliated with ECLA. Although I didn't remember ever meeting him before, I was told that he knew me and was glad that I would be working with him.

Now it became possible to legalize our residence in Argentina, clear our household effects through customs, and look for a new home. We found a nice little place in the northwestern suburbs with a large fireplace and a swimming pool that might have been a weekend retreat in former times. It was much nearer the American School, but now it was my turn to make the long commute to work. It wasn't so bad because a driver came from CONADE to pick me up so I could read papers on my way in. And then there was the compensation of living in a place surrounded by unpaved roads and open fields where I could go for a gallop early in the morning on the horse I soon bought – an early morning gallop does wonders to calm the frustrations of work! Our move was also healthy for another reason: only a couple of months later an explosion blew out the back of Sweet Home. It turned out that terrorists had been using one of the apartments to manufacture explosives.

My proposal for an economic recovery program was barely finished when the new head of CONADE finally arrived. We hit it off immediately and eventually became loyal friends. He was a statistician by profession and a serious technocrat like most of the economic team. One would never guess by his demeanor that he had been actively engaged in the underground bent on overthrowing Peron and had set off a bomb during one of the dictator's speeches in the Plaza de Mayo (the park in front of the Casa Rosada, the presidential palace). He had been captured and tortured, but he never spoke of this experience. Nor did his colleagues, most of whom had been active anti-Peronists too. They also shared a common turn of mind that I would describe as secretive, even a bit paranoid. I didn't fully appreciate until later the influence this bunker mentality would have on our efforts to strengthen the capacity of Argentine institutions for policy planning and analysis.

Our first task was to organize CONADE's new work program and to get the advisory project in full swing. We decided that the first item on the agenda should be preparation of a new five-year development plan. Argentina was committed under the Alliance for Progress to have such a plan, not for the purpose of strengthening government intervention in the economy but for orienting public policy and setting priorities for foreign assistance. No such effort had been made since the days of Peron, after whose ouster many records had been destroyed by revolutionaries intent on extirpating his heritage. Preparation of a national development plan therefore entailed a great deal of work to reconstruct records and improve the database.

The local staff of CONADE was well enough trained to gather the data needed to prepare a development plan, but with few exceptions they were not able to analyze it. This may seem strange in a well-educated country like Argentina, but local universities were just beginning to develop courses in modern economics. Contacts with the international academic community were virtually suspended during the Peron years, so most professionals of working age in the 1960s had been educated in the old oral tradition. They could speak intelligently and quote from the books they read, but they could not analyze empirical data and draw logical conclusions. What they wrote was seldom supported by the statistical evidence they assembled.

We therefore tried to recruit a resident advisory team with a lot of experience in practical policy analysis. Our monetary-fiscal expert was an Englishman who served as an adviser to the British treasury; for industrial development we chose an American who for many years had worked with the Puerto Rican government; and for agricultural adviser we recruited a Brazilian who had long experience as an international expert. The exception was an econometrician we hired from a Belgian university to help train our counterparts in quantitative analysis. This team of long-term resident advisers was supplemented by a longer list of short-term consultants. Many of them were university academics with special skills, such as Prof. Simon Kuznets, who helped our local colleagues revise Argentina's national accounts. Others were distinguished authorities in the formulation of public policy, such as Etienne Hirsch, the originator of "indicative" government planning in France.

The consultancy of M. Hirsch deserves special mention. He was selected in response to ongoing discussions I was having with counterparts on the role of national planning in a market economy. The previous planning experience of Argentina had been in a government-controlled economy, in which the state was responsible for directly allocating a large share of national resources. Indicative planning in France was mainly focused on forging a consensus between the public and private sectors to collaborate in fulfilling national development priorities. I thought that our Argentine colleagues should learn about a planning system that relied more on economic incentives and disincentives than on government directives and controls. M. Hirsch's visit also gave me an opportunity to dine in the Casa Rosada for the first time with the president, who was interested in consulting Hirsch about the forthcoming visit to Argentina by President Charles de Gaulle. His advice to Dr. Illia: be sure to engrave fleurs-de-lis on the dinnerware.

Recruiting appropriate foreign advisers and consultants is of course essential for the success of a technical assistance project; but selecting the right local support staff is also very important. We relied on CONADE personnel for secretarial and administrative services and luckily found a first class "fixer," the most critical member of the support staff. "Negro Britos," as this resourceful and out-going personality wanted to be called, really knew his way around the government bureaucracy: he could clear our things quickly through customs, rapidly obtain any necessary license or permit, and get me onto the tarmac at the airport to meet distinguished visitors, all for very modest gestures of friendship. The only person I hired from outside CONADE was a driver with mechanical skills to keep our locally assembled project car running. He was good at this daunting task, but he also seemed to have ambitions to race in the Indy 500. After he scared the wits out of the wife of one of our advisers, I regretfully had to dismiss him.

Perhaps the biggest challenge in organizing the project was to coordinate with other technical assistance missions. I have never been in a host country that did not have overlapping technical assistance projects, and Argentina was no exception: other foreign-funded experts were trying to help revise the national accounts, improve tax policy, measure unemployment, and develop human resources. These were all subjects that our own project was concerned with also. I could have urged the director of CONADE, who was responsible for coordinating all technical assistance and had asked my advice, to terminate these missions as unnecessary rivals to our own. But my attitude has always been that any one program of outside technical assistance, even if competent, is never sufficient to satisfy host country needs, especially in multidisciplinary areas such as education, public health, legal and information systems, and tax administration. I therefore tried to integrate these other technical assistance projects into our own work, despite allegations that I was "allowing foxes into the chicken coop." This criticism was repeated more forcefully when I later adopted the same attitude in Colombia.

All the necessary arrangements thus seemed finally in place for our advisory project with CONADE to proceed full steam ahead. We helped organize working groups to strengthen the database, review past performance of the economy sector by sector, and prepare diagnoses of the country's development problems. We organized in-house training seminars, prepared the first econometric model of the Argentine economy, and sent an outstanding local colleague to Harvard to complete his PhD.

It became increasingly clear, however, that CONADE, along with the rest of the economic team, was working almost in isolation. Contacts with the private business sector, which was accustomed to having access to the highest levels of government, were very limited. The same was true with most of organized labor, which was still controlled by Peronists who had been prevented from running their own candidate in the last presidential election. It also proved impossible to collaborate with local universities and research institutes, where most of the professional staff was not affiliated with the official party. CONADE didn't even have effective working relationships with key government ministries such as those responsible for public works and transportation, which were under the control of patronage appointees who owed no allegiance to the economic team.

The isolation of CONADE was clearly inconsistent with the indicative planning role I thought it should play to build a consensus between government and the private sector. The economic team didn't even take CONADE's work into account in formulating current economic policy, a shortcoming that threatened to make our longer-term planning efforts purely academic. So I tried to use my informal role as adviser to the economic team to forge a closer link between them and CONADE's policy planning and analysis staff.

When I prepared a draft of the economic section of the new president's first state-of-the-union message I based it on CONADE's recent work; and in a series of memos I submitted evidence to the Central Bank showing that the peso was becoming seriously overvalued and needed to be adjusted periodically to offset the 20 percent plus rate of domestic inflation.

It was personally flattering to hear the president repeat my words in his address to the nation, and I was gratified to see the Central Bank adopt a "crawling peg" exchange rate adjustment policy. But the trust the economic team apparently had in me did not carry over to the local staff. I was asked not to divulge my policy advisory work to anyone, not even to the staff of the Central Bank, which was presided over by the head of the economic team himself! This passion for secrecy, or what I previously referred to as a "bunker mentality," may have been justified to some extent by the very conflictual nature of Argentine society. Indeed, I have never seen politics conducted with such personal vindictiveness anywhere else except in Chile during the Allende-Pinochet period (although maybe we have approached this level at times in the United States, and seem to be doing so again). An environment of passionate distrust directed toward and among government officials, however, is not conducive to building highly respected public institutions with competent professional staffs.

Life on the home front, on the other hand, was not nearly so frustrating. We had our problems with public services such as telephone and electricity – it was easier to phone the U.S. than a neighbor across the street, and we had to keep cranking up our voltage booster every night to prevent our electric motors from burning out. Our horse was rustled, and Nacha fell victim to one of the aggressive local drivers; but Nacha found our horse again, and fortunately our car suffered most of the damage in the driving accident. Our daughters adjusted well to life in Argentina, despite being required to follow full courses of study in both Spanish and English simultaneously. Florel in fact won prizes as number one student in both languages at the American School. Nanine, on the other hand, turned into a cowgirl and spent most of her time every afternoon on horseback galloping around the neighborhood.

Among our most memorable experiences were the personal friendships we developed with Argentines. We virtually became members of a couple of families, who helped us understand a great deal about local customs and life styles. One of our friends taught Argentine folk music to my three women, who became quite proficient playing the guitar and singing together in several parts (they allowed me to accompany them on the *bombo* or drum). One aspect of Argentine life we were never able to adjust to fully, however, was that almost everything happened late. Many of the day's most important activities didn't even begin until nightfall. The streets of Buenos Aires were filled with whole families walking around until midnight, and adult night life didn't really start until one or two o'clock in the morning. This nocturnal predilection probably explained why most employees didn't turn up at CONADE until after 10 A.M. and why important substantive meetings were usually held during what I called "Kremlin hours," namely after administrative and junior personnel left the office to attend evening concerts, lectures, and coffee house rendezvous.

By 1965 CONADE completed most of its work on the five-year development plan, but it was becoming increasingly doubtful whether the plan would ever be implemented. Opposition to the regime, especially from influential business and financial interests, was growing more strident. By the end of the year, rumors of a coup d'état began to circulate. I therefore concluded that the time had come to broaden the reach of our project beyond government circles to Argentine professionals of diverse political persuasions. My counterpart, Sr. Carranza, agreed to start distributing CONADE studies to the general public, and I arranged speaking engagements with various organizations to discuss development issues highlighted in our work. These outreach efforts and publication of the final plan document were in general well received, and I am convinced that they helped CONADE survive after the coup d'état finally occurred in mid-1966.

The coup was fortunately almost bloodless, unlike previous Argentine revolutions. On this occasion the military simply walked into the Casa Rosada without opposition and ushered President Illia out. Nacha and I were not aware of this, however, because we were attending a DAS conference in Italy at the time. When word of the coup reached us there, we were at first immensely concerned about the safety of our daughters, who had remained in Buenos Aires. One of our good Argentine friends had agreed to move in with them while we were away, however, so we were confident that they were in good hands. But it was a great relief when our friend assured us by phone that everything was peaceful.

I now had to decide what to do with our project under the new military government. One alternative was to resign under protest, to make a big splash against military dictatorship, as some of my colleagues urged. But I considered this posture to be quite inappropriate – I felt strongly that foreign advisers should not intervene in the internal politics of a host country. So we did not terminate our project immediately but instead cut back assistance gradually until early 1967, when the project finally came to an end. Harvard might have been able to negotiate an extension of the project under the new military regime, but my personal loyalty to the former economic team precluded this possibility. I urged Argentine professional staff to remain in CONADE, however, arguing that continuity of personnel would help strengthen the institutionalization of technical staff organizations in government.

The DiTella Institute was not directly affected by the turmoil, although a few of their economists joined the economic team of the new military government. But our advisory project was not working out as expected: not only did it prove impossible to involve the institute in contract research with government, but most of its senior economists were still engaged in preparing their PhD dissertations. Because this work was supervised by thesis advisers in various universities abroad, the role of DAS advisers in strengthening the technical capacity of the institute was marginal. When the DAS decided to suspend the CONADE project, it also agreed to withdraw from DiTella.

Our departure from Argentina at the end of 1966 was very emotional. Argentine friends showered us with gifts to help remember them: albums of Argentine folk music, a dictionary of Argentine slang (*lumfardo*), a guitar from our CONADE driver, etc. I was also written up in the second lead article of *Primera Plana*, the national news magazine, which portrayed me as a kind of Rasputin, the economic power behind the Illia regime. And a business gossip magazine even alleged that I was a communist spy who had tried to infiltrate the government with leftist ideology. This unexpected publicity raised in my mind the question of whether I had made a mistake in playing such a high profile role as a government adviser, and of whether our institution-building efforts might be viewed instead as just another imperialist intrigue to foist foreign ideas on the country.

Chapter V ∼

Revitalization of the Colombia Project

*B*y 1966 our advisory project with the National Planning Department (DNP) in Colombia was languishing, virtually ignored by the government and without competent local staff. Most of our advisers had already departed when I was asked to make a short visit to Bogotá late in the year to see what could be done to revive the project. Good luck accompanied me again: the recently elected president, Carlos Lleras Restrepo, was keen on building a strong professional team and had just appointed a good friend of mine as head of the DNP. Edgar Gutierrez had been a Public Service Fellow at Harvard when I directed the program, and both he and his wife had become quite close to our family.

The first problem we had to face together in his new job was how to help him pay income tax on his previous year's earnings in the private sector, which had been much larger than his new government salary. Colombia happened to be one of the few Latin countries where the obligation to pay income taxes was taken more seriously. Even President Lleras was in a bind for the same reason, but he was able to collect donations from political supporters to help pay his tax obligations. Edgar could not tap the same source, so the director of the DAS and I lent him the necessary funds from our own pockets. This was a risky way to begin an adviser-counterpart relationship, but it turned out well as Edgar paid back his loan conscientiously.

A much more difficult problem to solve was how to revitalize the DNP. Few qualified Colombians were interested in joining an organization with so little prestige and credibility, so we had to find ways to make the DNP a more attractive place to work. Edgar therefore moved the organization to handsome new quarters and negotiated some improvements in staff salaries and benefits, while I arranged for several well-known international experts on economic development to come to Colombia to speak at widely publicized conferences sponsored by the DNP. At the end of each conference all participants and DNP professional staff would be invited to a reception at the presidential palace together with prominent government officials.

The most important part of our revitalization strategy was to change the mission of the DNP. Up to this time the department had been engaged mainly in preparing a five-year development plan, which as in Argentina was an obligation under the Alliance for Progress. In contrast to Argentina, however, there was no urgent need to reconstruct records and improve the database, and a number of studies had already been carried out on key development issues. So Edgar and I persuaded the president to convert the organization into a kind of technical secretariat of the newly formed National

Florel dancing with Dad at her "coming of age" party, 1966

Economic and Social Policy Council (CONPES). This was a cabinet level body that met regularly under the chairmanship of the president himself to design and discuss current national policies. We were convinced that this new role would make the DNP a much more attractive, even an exciting, place to work.

With the revitalization strategy underway, I now turned my attention to moving the family to Bogotá for a short period. We wanted our girls to return to school in the U.S. again by the fall of 1967, when Florel would be entering eleventh grade. Not many landlords were willing to rent their houses for less than a year, but fortunately a local DNP staff member who was away on training abroad agreed to let us use his home. It came with two maids and a dog named Napo (short for Napoleon), who obviously was an important member of the family. The arrangement worked out okay even though Nacha was allergic to bites from Napo's fleas and was terrified when he got into fights with dogs three times his size. The girls' education didn't suffer, because they found space in the local American school.

*Nanine
with Dad in
Cartagena,
Colombia,
1967*

Colombia has a reputation for being a rather dangerous place to live, but in the late 1960s things were pretty tranquil. One was still warned to keep car windows closed at stoplights to avoid having rings and watches ripped off, and to keep a firm grip on one's wallet in open markets. But there was little political violence and the co-caine industry had not started yet. Public services were also reason-ably well managed – the phones usually worked and it wasn't neces-sary to have a voltage booster. The main dangers came from Mother Nature in the form of volcanic eruptions, landslides, and earthquakes. But Nacha and I were accustomed to such dangers, having been brought up in Chile and California respectively, although a really big tremor hit Bogotá while we lived there. Fortunately, the results were more humorous than life threatening: the wife of a newly arrived ad-viser, who was having a cocktail when she was thrown to the floor, thereafter marveled at the potency of local alcoholic beverages; and Nacha, who was taking a shower when the quake struck, thought she was getting old prematurely when she had to clutch the curtain to avoid falling down.

Back on the job I was pleased to see that our revitalization strat-egy was producing desired results. The conferences by international experts succeeded in drawing distinguished crowds, and the recep-tions at the presidential palace proved to be a real morale booster for DNP's professional staff. They also had their comical moments, par-ticularly when John Kenneth Galbraith came to town. He is over six and a half feet tall, so when he was introduced to the petite Presi-dent Lleras at one of the receptions, the president craned his neck uncomfortably to look him in the face and insisted that he sit on a low stool to converse. Ken was writing a novel at the time and asked to be taken to Cartagena on the Caribbean coast to gather local color, so we had to scramble to get a small plane to fly him there and back on the same day. Our project therefore deserves some of the credit for helping Professor Galbraith boast that he later had both fiction and non-fiction books on the *New York Times* best seller list at the same time.

The DNP-sponsored conferences led by international experts clearly helped to enhance the poor image of the organization, but the main at-

Nacha at orchid nursery in Colombia, 1967

traction for qualified Colombians to join the staff was the department's new role as technical secretariat of CONPES. The DNP was placed in charge of organizing the agenda of council meetings in consultation with the president. It then prepared position papers on agenda topics, solicited comments on the papers from various government ministries and agencies, and submitted memos to the council summarizing diverse positions on issues to facilitate debate and policy decision-making. Effective performance of this secretariat function soon led to additional assignments for the DNP, such as designing the reform of foreign investment regulations and managing a fund for financing the preparation and evaluation of government investment projects. The DNP was rapidly becoming the chief technical staff agency of the Colombian government.

For all of these activities, DAS advisers and consultants participated actively in the preparation and discussion of strategies, studies, and memos. They also led internal training seminars and even helped teach local university courses to allow counterparts with academic responsibilities to devote more time to their work at the DNP. The type of resident DAS adviser appropriate for providing this kind of techni-

Typical street market in Colombia

cal assistance was quite different from what we needed in Argentina. Instead of senior experts chosen for their practical policy-advising experience, we recruited more junior, academically oriented advisers who could more easily bond with their counterparts on an intellectual level.

The university-type environment we helped create in the DNP had its drawbacks too. For example, one of our advisers (ironically from another Latin American country) took his semi-academic role too seriously and marked his memos "do not quote without permission of the author." The major practical drawback of our adviser-recruiting policy, however, confirmed that old adage that familiarity breeds contempt: local counterparts did not think that the help they received from their foreign colleagues of similar age justified the difference in salary levels. They of course were right in believing that local salaries were inadequate, but they were wrong in thinking that the same amount of money spent on academic training of Colombians abroad would be more beneficial for strengthening their institution than the on-the-job training they were receiving. This is a topic that will be discussed more thoroughly in the next chapter.

One of the restrictions I imposed on our advisers also probably contributed to weakening local counterpart perception of the worth of their foreign colleagues: I strictly forbade any adviser including myself to attend a CONPES meeting. It was my firm belief that locals should be directly responsible for making policy decisions in their own country. Foreigners who become embroiled in local politics may be successful for a while, but sooner or later they become rivals of local politicians for power and influence and lose credibility as independent professional experts. In this decision I was also influenced by the negative effect of my high-profile role in Argentina: instead of helping to incorporate local counterparts in policy making, I replaced them. Policy makers preferred to turn to me personally for advice, bypassing the very institution that we were trying to build up. I am still convinced that there is no way to teach people to be responsible without giving them responsibilities and then holding them accountable for results.

My restriction on advisers attending CONPES meetings was strongly resisted initially by our local counterparts themselves. They of course would have felt more secure if their foreign colleagues helped them defend jointly prepared position papers before the president and his ministers. But after some stumblings and a few embarrassments, most of the professional staff learned how to do the job well and rapidly gained confidence; those who could not were left by the wayside, another very important part of the process of building professionally competent institutions.

DAS advisers and consultants did not, of course, remain glued to their desks in the DNP as a result of my restriction. With their counterparts they attended meetings at the highest level in their areas of responsibility, and a few short-term experts even appeared before CONPES to report on new research findings on issues of special interest to the government. We also helped organize a very high-profile international commission, led by Professor Musgrave of Harvard, to reform the Colombian tax system. As project director I was furthermore responsible for keeping abreast of the activities of international organizations in Colombia. I was requested by the president to attend several meetings he had with missions from international financial agencies, and I was again involved in helping to coordinate foreign technical assistance from other sources, as I had done in Argentina.

By the fall of 1967 our new resident advisory team was well settled in, and the project seemed to be moving ahead as smoothly as could be expected. It seemed to me that my physical presence in Bogotá was no longer necessary, and that it was good time to return to Harvard to refresh my energies and to take stock of what I had been doing. After more than four years living abroad, it was also time for the girls to return to the States for their secondary education, which in general was not of the same quality in American schools overseas. Perhaps even more important, it would be healthy for them to socialize with a more diverse group of peers, who play such a vital role in the life of teenagers. Almost all of the peers they associated with in American schools abroad belonged to an elite composed of the diplomatic corps, so-called "military brats," and wealthy local families.

The change, I thought, would also be very healthy for Nacha. During the last four years she had devoted her life almost exclusively to being the alter ego of a project director (aside of course from being a mother). This wifely role is little understood and seldom appreciated. It consists, in addition to being a sounding board and chief adviser to her husband, of assisting other advisers' families to settle into a new environment, identifying their problems and helping them find solutions, being her husband's social secretary, organizing and presiding over events for visiting dignitaries, and many other activities that contribute to the success of her husband's work. It was ripe time that Nacha was given the opportunity again to pursue her own professional interests.

So back we went to Newton to buy a new home and re-establish some semblance of roots for the family. In some ways it was like going to another foreign country – protests were escalating about the war in Vietnam, and new teenage lifestyles had emerged that we did not fully comprehend. Settling in back home turned out to be almost as much of a challenge as starting a new advisory project abroad.

CHAPTER VI ∾
TAKING STOCK

We returned to Boston in time for our daughters to enter school in the fall of 1967. Florel was already approaching 16 and Nanine was two and a half years younger, but they had spent barely three years of their lives so far residing in the U.S. We were determined now to remain in the States until they finished secondary school and went off to college, even though I had to commute frequently to Bogotá until a new project director was appointed. We also wanted to invite my father, a widower living alone in Los Angeles, to come live with us. So we bought a house large enough to accommodate all of our needs – three bedrooms, three baths, a study for me, and a basement playroom for the girls – again in Newton. We still live there.

We had hardly settled into our new home, however, when I began to receive offers to go elsewhere. It appears that I had become some kind of celebrity in international development circles: several international organizations offered me jobs, the Brookings Institution wanted me to go to Washington as a visiting scholar, ECLA asked whether I would be interested in becoming deputy executive director, and I was written up in *Who's Who*.

It may not have been the best decision for advancing my career, but we decided to reject these offers and stay in Newton, mainly for the girls' sake but also because I liked my job. I was looking forward to taking stock of what I had been doing, recharging my intellectual batteries at Harvard, and writing a book based on my Argentine experience.

Nacha was also looking forward to professional work again, and she eventually landed a job as director of bilingual education in the Framingham public schools. The flood of immigrant children entering Massachusetts schools at the time was not of course restricted to a single town or to Spanish speakers, so with the help of a federal grant Nacha founded a multilanguage center to serve Framingham and surrounding communities. She was also appointed to the state

Bilingual Commission and was invited to give lectures on the subject in a number of local colleges and universities. It was clearly not the right time for the Mallon family to move away from Boston.

The director of the DAS agreed, so I became an academic again, teaching some courses at Harvard and starting my book. I got a grant from the Social Science Research Council to bring a former CONADE colleague, Juan Sourrouille, to Harvard to help me with the research, and within a couple of years the book was ready for publication by Harvard University Press. The Spanish version of the book was later published in Argentina and soon became a standard text in local universities there. The title was *Policy-Making in a Conflict Society: The Argentine Case*.

During preparation of the book I was able to reflect a great deal on our advisory experience in Argentina. Both the CONADE and the DiTella Institute projects could be considered unsuccessful: they ended abruptly without achieving their institution-building objectives. If we had known more about DiTella and the difficulty of obtaining government research contracts before we started the project, we probably would not have undertaken it at all. Institute personnel already had numerous contacts with universities abroad, so they really didn't need the DAS to help them identify qualified foreign research collaborators. And having a resident DAS adviser experienced in negotiating and managing government research contracts would have been useless too.

The same cannot be said about the CONADE project: I still think it was well conceived and designed. The problem was that at the outset we did not understand the difficulties of strengthening government staff organizations in such a conflictual society. Had we understood at the beginning, I could have spent less time trying to insert CONADE into the policy-making process and more time disseminating the results of our work to a broader constituency, as I tried to do later. But such a strategy would almost certainly have been counterproductive: a national policy analysis and planning agency that is cut off from the policy-making process makes no sense. If it survived, it would simply become another academic research institution and would never attract the kind of policy-oriented professionals that our project was intended to help train.

Even though the project did come to an end rather abruptly, I think it finally achieved many of the objectives we set out to accomplish. After languishing for several months following the coup d'état while the new government tried to get its bearings, CONADE was revived by one of our friends when he became economics minister. He appointed as the new director a young Harvard PhD who proceeded to turn the Council into an effective policy analysis and planning agency. Even the econometric model we helped develop was used to design the most successful stabilization and adjustment program the country had had up to that time.

I think our project also had a still more significant long-term impact. A number of CONADE colleagues later occupied prominent government positions as ministers and agency heads; and a decade and a half later Juan Sourrouille, the co-author of my book, became the economics minister with the longest tenure in Argentine history. "People building," I firmly believe, is in the long run a more important part of institution building than is strengthening any particular organization. People are less ephemeral than bureaucracies, which tend to keep changing over time to adapt to new conditions and to satisfy the need of political newcomers to redesign government in their own image.

In contrast to our projects in Argentina, the one in Colombia was generally considered a great success by the time I returned to Harvard. The DNP in fact became a model for government policy analysis and planning organizations in other Latin American countries to emulate. As the local DNP staff became stronger and more self-confident, however, they began to lose interest in continued DAS advisory assistance. The source of funding for the project also shifted from the Ford Foundation to the Inter-American Development Bank, which I think felt a bit awkward financing a gringo resident advisory group. So when the leadership of the DNP changed after the election of a new president at the end of the 1960s, the government agreed with the IADB to terminate the project.

Termination of the project at a time when the DNP was prospering could be considered another sign of success. Foreign advisers are after all supposed to work themselves out of a job. But I think this termination was premature; our project could have been redesigned to provide more sophisticated assistance that would have been very beneficial to the DNP. As backstopper of the project in Harvard, I should have been more alert to the changing situation in Colombia and taken more initiative to redesign the project, but I was absorbed in academic work and writing my book on Argentina. As an educator, however, it was inexcusable for me to forget that one cannot teach the same course year after year without updating the content. I suspect that other providers of technical assistance are prone to making the same mistake.

Our DNP project was also criticized for not intervening more forcefully in policy formation. Lauchlin Currie, a prominent economist who led the first World Bank mission to Colombia in 1950 and remained there to work during most of the rest of his career, lauded our success in turning the DNP around in his book, *The Role of Economic Advisers in Developing Countries*: "A complete reversal had occurred from the first three and a half years of the Harvard Mission. Both agency and mission now occupied a highly favorable, indeed privileged, position" (p.80). But then he added

> The evaluation report of the Harvard-Colombia Advisory Group submitted by Richard Mallon in March 1968 contained *not a word on policy*. The evaluation was exclusively concerned with training... despite the fact that in the previous fifteen months, the periodic reports of the mission had listed no less than 120 memoranda by title, many dealing with policies or with matters having policy implications... (that)... can also be found in DNP memoranda submitted to CONPES. (pp. 81 and 86)

Currie was truly a policy activist like Richard Gilbert in Pakistan; and he practiced what he preached by playing a high-profile role in promoting his own development strategy when he later became chief adviser to the DNP himself. As a *de facto* member of the government economic team, his tenure as well as his strategy not surprisingly lasted only until the next election, when a new economic team came to power. This is what all high-profile advisers should expect to happen: when a new military faction took over in Pakistan in 1968, the high profile of Richard Gilbert became a political liability and the DAS advisory project was terminated two years later. It happened again in Ghana in 1972 when the currency devaluation forcefully advocated by DAS advisers led to a change of government and the suspension of the project.

Policy advocacy also can create divisions among the advisers themselves. The ethnic riots of 1969 in Malaysia split the DAS advisory group down the middle between those advisers supporting and those opposing the New Economic Policy adopted by the government, which gave preference to indigenous Malays over citizens of Chinese ancestry.

There is of course nothing wrong with policy advocacy and policy disagreements among advisers. On the contrary, vigorous policy discussions among advisers and counterparts, in which sound reasoning and analysis are valued more than rank and seniority, are an essential part of effective in-service training. This is what we tried to do in Colombia. It is quite another matter when advisers push a common "party line" within the advisee organization. And if they go outside of the organization to push their policy agendas, foreign advisers become participants in the national arena where the outcome of policy debates is determined as much or more by political power and influence as by sound reasoning and analysis. Advisers competing (even at times with their own counterparts) for political power and policy influence are not likely to devote much of their time to in-service training. As Currie himself concluded in the book previously cited, "In contrasting the length, size and sponsorship of the [DAS advisory] mission with the rather meager [policy] results obtained, one is forced to concur... that the results hardly justified the effort. For training, money spent in foreign scholarships pays higher dividends" (p.86).

This statement is, in my opinion, based on a very simplistic comparison of the costs and benefits of taking students to the teachers vs. taking teachers to the students. The comparison would be valid only if two methods for providing the same kind of education were being evaluated. But university education in the social sciences is highly specialized at the graduate or professional level and emphasizes the learning of basic theory and analytical techniques in a specific discipline. In-service training in policy planning and analysis, on the other hand, is interdisciplinary in focus and stresses the practical application of analytical tools in a wide variety of situations in which experience and good judgment are often more useful than academic rigor. Foreign and in-service training are really complementary blades of the same scissors. Graduate university education abroad is best suited for preparing professors and researchers who in turn can give good basic training to budding policy analysts in *local* educational and research institutions. After these budding policy analysts receive intensive in-service training on the job, the outstanding ones can profitably upgrade their skills by participating in mid-career educational programs abroad such as the Mason Fellow program at Harvard, which is specifically designed for this purpose. The opportunity to participate in such programs can also be used to at-tract some of the best local talent to the organizations we advise.

That on-the-job training is more effective than formal education to prepare people for specific jobs is supported by abundant empiri-cal evidence. For example, various studies carried out on the results of the Job Training Partnership Act in the U.S., the Youth Training program in Britain, and other such programs that rely on schoolroom training reveal that graduates are no better at finding jobs than the general population. In contrast, studies of apprenticeship programs in countries such as Germany and Spain have shown that on-the-job training brings clear improvements in productivity and wages. Indeed, John Dewey's concept of "learning-by-doing" has been applied suc-cessfully in many areas of education for generations.

Very well and good, replied the Ford Foundation in effect, but are U.S. university advisory groups in Latin America really providing the kind of in-service training you advocate? And even if they are, the foundation continued, why does in-service training still require for-eigners now that local experts are becoming increasingly available in Latin America? Very legitimate questions, I responded, so why don't we take a look at what's actually going on in the field? The founda-tion therefore agreed to send me to Chile with two other social scien-tists to evaluate a couple of ongoing advisory projects they financed there. I couldn't go to Chile, of course, without taking my family with me, so off we flew together as soon as the girls were out of school. Little did I anticipate that the consequences of this trip would be just as important for our family as they were for my profession.

Nacha and I were worried that our teenage daughters could be bored if they only spent time with her extended family in Chile, so one of my Chilean students at Harvard arranged for us to have them meet a brother-in-law of his who had just graduated from medical school. Nanine, who was always standing on tiptoe to be as mature as her older sister, fell madly in love and announced later that she was determined to marry him. The affair continued for a long time with much discussion until we finally, with grave reservations, consented to her marriage after she graduated from high school, with one con-dition: she would not have any children until she finished college.

Nanine and her new husband moved to nearby Worcester, where she enrolled in Clark University to major in her preferred field of psychology while he completed his medical internship and residency in local hospitals. She fulfilled her promise by accelerating her studies and receiving her B.A. diploma in a state of advanced pregnancy, while two old ladies nearby clicked their tongues disapprovingly at the graduation ceremony. As we had feared, the marriage eventually ended in divorce, but not until she gave us two cherished grandsons.

The projects we were asked to evaluate in Chile were managed by two different U.S. universities to provide technical assistance for urban planning in one case and for national development policy analysis in the other. We found that neither project fulfilled our expectations. One of them was led by a charismatic, high-profile adviser who, we concluded in our report, "used the need of a host country for sound guidance and advice as an opportunity to apply broad and untested social hypotheses" and to spell out "the implications of preconceived solutions to problems." Advisers working with the other project were serious scholars, but they were engaged in long-term research that ignored the reality that "research efforts must begin to have a pretty rapid payoff in terms of operational policy guidance if the organization being advised is to maintain (or develop) an important role in the government bureaucracy." The kind of practical in-service training I had in mind could hardly be provided by advisers peddling a "party line" or absorbed in academic research.

This experience led me to pursue more vigorously an idea I had been developing for some time; namely, that it would be better to provide technical assistance to policy planning and analysis organizations through a consortium of U.S. and Latin American universities and research institutions. This approach would make it more difficult for an advisory group to pursue a single party line, and the incorporation of more Latin experts in the process might deflect rising nationalistic objections to foreign assistance. It may have been like trying to push cooked spaghetti to embark on such an ambitious and complex plan, but the Ford Foundation went along and agreed to finance my visits to several universities and a large conference I organized at Harvard at the end of 1970. The results of the conference were probably predictable, at least with hindsight now that I look back more than a quarter of a century later.

Latin American institutions were clearly set on maintaining their "independence" and picking their own foreign collaborators should they need them, and elite U.S. universities were becoming increasingly doubtful about the advisability of assuming responsibility for any technical assistance abroad. The view that universities are a national resource subject to public call was undergoing critical reevaluation, partly because of the questionable contribution of public service activities to regular teaching and research and because of the lack of involvement of most university academics in such activities.

Harvard University's review of the DAS published in the so-called Dorfman Report had come to the same conclusion a year earlier, namely that the DAS was rather remote from the university and did not generate cutting-edge research. In its own report issued in March 1971, the Ford Foundation noted this conflict between the advisory responsibilities of the DAS and the pressure to devote more attention to research. The foundation's report concluded that although "the quality of advisers for overseas projects of the DAS has been remarkably high compared to similar technical assistance missions," too little local training was carried out. Ford therefore decided that its money could be better spent directly on training instead of through foreign advisory groups. The withdrawal of the foundation from financing DAS projects, almost half of the cost of which they had funded up to this time, was a very severe blow to the organization.

The blows seemed to be coming from every side, both at the professional and personal levels. Not only were the Pakistan and Colombia projects terminated at this time, but also in Liberia the UNDP decided to suspend the DAS advisory project and instead hire foreign experts directly. Back home, Harvard students were rebelling against U.S. involvement in the Vietnam war and, together with radical faculty members, targeting other University international programs including those of the DAS. Florel, who had enrolled in Radcliffe College, joined the student protest movement and approached me to write an "exposé" of the DAS for the *Harvard Crimson*, the student newspaper, but she wisely desisted after considering possible conflicts of interest. My father decided to abandon our home and return to Los Angeles to spend his last years, and a tornado struck our vacation home in Maine, draping large trees over the roof and causing extensive damage.

So this period of taking stock ended with the feeling that everything was coming apart. The withdrawal of the Ford Foundation from financing DAS projects meant that the in-service training and institution-building emphasis of our work, with which I personally identified, would be subordinated to the priorities of other funders of technical assistance. The pressure of the university to generate more rigorous academic research, which I thought most development advisers including myself were not inclined or well qualified to carry out, would be intensified. And some of my students, including one of my own daughters, felt that what I was doing represented illegitimate interference in the internal affairs of poor countries.

Taking stock at mid career was thus a sobering experience. A couple of my colleagues decided to abandon ship, but I never seriously considered leaving the DAS. In fact, I felt rather excited by the challenge of looking for new funders and agendas that would allow me to maintain a low profile and to continue emphasizing in-service training and people-building. In so doing I didn't think that I could be fairly accused of interfering in the internal affairs of host countries. I was also reasonably confident that Harvard would recognize that this kind of advisory work was a legitimate educational activity that enriched applied research and teaching at the University, at least in the professional schools if not in the Faculty of Arts and Sciences.

Some readers of an earlier draft of these memoirs commented that I must have been more shaken up and depressed by these events than I admit. Perhaps I am what is sometimes called an "invulnerable" who refuses to accept defeat, who considers that past disappointments and future uncertainties are part of life's inevitable challenges to test one's mettle. It also certainly helped to have a spouse like mine who always gave me full support. In any event, I was ready to start the next leg of my journey without a destination.

Chapter VII ~
New Funders and Agendas

*N*ow that our daughters were no longer at home, it was time again to look for an overseas assignment, this time during a period of great uncertainty. Would new funders be interested in financing technical assistance for the in-service training and institution building in national policy planning and analysis that the Ford Foundation had supported in the past and that I felt qualified to provide? Would the revolutionary fervor that was sweeping Latin America in the 1970s create an especially hostile environment for foreign advisers? And what would be the impact of the oil shocks that caused petroleum prices to skyrocket and triggered a lending frenzy by multinational banks hard-pressed to recycle the huge inflow of petro-dollar deposits?

Peruvian Sojourn Funded by the UNDP

These questions were uppermost in my mind when I received an invitation from a former student to investigate a project in Peru, which had just undergone a revolutionary change of government and was expecting a big increase in petroleum exports. The project was to be financed by the United Nations Development Program (UNDP) and was intended to help create a "think tank" for policy analysis and research in the National Planning Institute (INP) in Lima. The INP had been chosen by the new nationalist military regime to assist in defining a middle road between capitalism and state socialism. The initial actions of the regime after taking power from a moderate but rather ineffective government were to nationalize the principal multinational petroleum company, carry out a sweeping land reform, and introduce a system of labor participation in the ownership and management of private business.

Although clearly left of center politically, this regime resembled that of President Cardenas in Mexico during the 1930s more than the national populist dictatorship of Peron in Argentina in the 1940s. Peruvian military leaders did not appear to be motivated by a lust for personal power so much as by revulsion against the violent repression they had been ordered to carry out against discontented Indian and mestizo groups in the poverty-stricken highlands and urban coastal slums. Many army officials came from this same background and identified personally with these groups more than with the white elite that traditionally ran the country. They were convinced that if radical changes were not made in the way the economy was organized, class warfare would eventually overwhelm the country and bring to power a Peruvian Fidel Castro, or, from their point of view, even a worse leader (the *Sendero Luminoso* or Shining Path movement did not exist yet, but violent protests by other dissident groups were on the rise).

Despite considerable misgivings about how a gringo could work effectively in this kind of environment, I accepted the challenge and spent the summers of 1971 and 1972 directing a small DAS mission to explore the possibility of establishing a longer term advisory relationship with the INP. My first impression of the INP was positive. The general in charge of the institute did not interfere in the substantive work of the staff, which was composed of reasonably competent professionals of every conceivable political stripe, from a couple of marxists to a Jesuit priest who was working on his PhD thesis in economics from a university in Boston. The technical director, who looked like an Incan nobleman, and most other senior staff were very open and easy to work with. I was also quite impressed by the desire of the institute to promote collaborative research with local universities and research institutes.

We started by poring over background documents prepared by the INP and other agencies to familiarize ourselves with the socioeconomic situation in Peru and to identify researchable topics. We also spread out to interview researchers in the universities and other organizations to find out what they were doing and to sound out their interest in possible collaboration. And then we organized a series of seminars to discuss topics our colleagues found of special interest, and we attended staff meetings to review the institute's work. We were actually beginning to feel like regular staff members, especially when my counterparts began to bring me government policy papers, some marked "confidential," for my comments. When I questioned the propriety of showing such documents to a foreigner, they shrugged and said that the military even stamped "confidential" on the toilet paper in the bathrooms.

By and by it became clear that I was being encouraged to raise controversial issues that my chief counterparts wanted raised while they appeared to remain neutral between the very diverse points of view expressed by institute staff. They even assigned responsibility for research on population control to the Jesuit priest so that the views of the Church might be voiced (his half-humorous response was, "What will my bishop say?" but he proved how ecumenical he really was by refusing to be released by terrorists during their occupation of the Japanese Embassy many years later so that he could administer to the needs of kidnappers and kidnapped alike). Once all the issues were on the table, I guessed that my chief counterparts would then take a stand when they saw which way the political winds were blowing at the policy-making level. If this was their strategy, my advisory role was presumably to call the shots as I saw them, and discuss them with the staff, but not press my own policy opinions unless the leadership asked me to.

I particularly remember trying to play this role in a large INP staff meeting on short-term planning. At one point I observed that state ownership of business enterprises did not require adoption of a centrally planned command economy, which in fact had proved unworkable in Eastern Europe and India. I said that trying to control an economy with centralized government directives was just as fruitless as trying to straighten out cooked spaghetti so that it could be pushed. I could see by his expression that at least one senior staff member seemed disturbed by my observation. After the meeting my chief counterparts commended me on making an important point and suggested that I go to the displeased staff member's office to talk it over.

I found out that he had been trained at the University of Louvain in Belgium, the home of "liberation theology" where economics was apparently taught as a branch of moral philosophy – economic relationships should be governed by principles of social justice, not by impersonal competitive markets. I tried to explain that this was a practical issue of economic management, that even socialist countries were attempting to introduce more market incentives to reduce the bureaucratic inefficiencies of centralized government controls. I doubt that I convinced him to alter his convictions, but I think we parted with greater mutual respect and a touch of humor. He said that he had been offended mainly by the levity of my comment and the implications of my using the expression "*harden* cooked spaghetti so that it could be pushed" (in a slip of the tongue I had used the

word *endurecer* or "harden" instead of *enderezar* or "straighten out").
Oh, the pitfalls of trying to make jokes in a foreign language!

My chief counterparts also wanted me to provide advice on foreign technical assistance. As was (and would be) the case in all the countries I worked, many foreign agencies were already providing or proposing to provide technical assistance to the country. These included: various foreign universities, the United Nations, the Organization of American States, the Inter-American Development Bank, ILPES (the international training and consulting institute attached to ECLA in Santiago), the Ford Foundation, etc. The INP was placed in charge of sorting it all out, so I was first asked to comment on Ford's proposal to finance a study of graduate training in economics at local universities.

This request was rather ironic given my previous close association with the Ford Foundation and especially in view of a note from Ford I found in the files. It said in part, "The Foundation desires to make clear that the use of the services of the DAS ... (for which it is magnificently prepared) should not be interpreted as an indication that the foundation necessarily would support a contract with the DAS... Perhaps it would be wise to consider also the recruitment of consultants from other Latin American sources such as the DiTella Institute in Buenos Aires or other Latin American institutions." (Where had I heard this before?)

It was probably my involvement in advising the INP on technical assistance that motivated the UNDP resident representative to grant me special privileges not included in my contract. During a long weekend holiday he provided me with a Land Rover to explore the Altiplano (high plateau) and the fringe of the Amazon basin with one of my adviser colleagues. It was a trip I shall never forget: viewing Indian villages snuggled on terraced mountainsides, attending a local festival with two competing musical bands blasting away on opposite sides of the plaza, spending the night on the floor of an ancient Franciscan monastery, changing a flat tire on a mountain road with rocks rolling by from a landslide, navigating a narrow, winding dirt road with a thousand foot drop on one side. I also wanted to see for myself what was happening with the land reform, so we climbed up to a remote ranch situated at over 11,000 feet.

At this altitude even cattle had difficulty breathing, so the ranch was dedicated mainly to sheep raising. Most of the managers had worked for the former private owner, but now they were enthusiastically trying to reinvest profits to raise productivity and diversify output. The main obstacle, they said, was that the new owners were more interested in paying off their debt to the government so that they could become sole proprietors as quickly as possible. Little money was left over for reinvesting in the property. Similar problems with incentives under the new systems of ownership and management appeared to be quite widespread, not only in agriculture but also in business enterprises.

Upon my return to Lima I therefore raised the subject with my chief counterparts. They told me that they were aware of the problem and that they had requested technical assistance from the Soviet Union or an Eastern European country, which might be able to share its experience. None of the current providers of technical assistance, however, had been able to identify such an expert – possibly for ideological reasons, my counterparts suspected. So I proposed that the DAS contract an internationally respected expert from Yugoslavia, a country that had extensive experience in the field of labor ownership and management of enterprises. My counterparts approved after reviewing his credentials, which included regular stints as visiting professor at Harvard (where he shocked his students by explaining how the federal government exercised more control over the economy in the U.S. than in his own country). The success of his visit, added to other backstopping services the DAS provided by making available useful bibliographical and documentary materials the INP needed, helped consolidate our relationship.

Partly for this reason perhaps, the UNDP representative decided to provide me with a personal car for daily use in Lima. It came in very handy when my family arrived for a visit, and especially when Florel came to carry out exploratory research for her undergraduate honors thesis on Latin American history and literature. In addition to pursuing her own research, Florel also found time to help me with my public relations. I remember in particular the time when she represented me at the funeral of the wife of the INP technical director (the "Incan nobleman") while I was away on a trip outside of Lima during the second summer of my mission. The technical director's grief and depression may have had something to do with the final outcome of our efforts to organize a longer-term advisory project with the INP.

Negotiation of a longer-term contract with the INP was one of the main objectives of our advisory mission in the summer of 1972. My chief INP counterparts seemed to be strongly in favor, and so did the UNDP representative. But suddenly a serious obstacle surfaced: UNDP advisory contracts with outside consultants contained a secrecy-of-information clause that was unacceptable to Harvard lawyers concerned about protecting academic freedom. The only way out seemed to be for the DAS to enter into a subcontract with a UN-affiliated institution such as ILPES that did not include the objectionable clause. So I decided to fly to Santiago, Chile, to discuss the possibility of technical assistance collaboration with Raul Prebisch, who was then the Executive Director of ILPES. We reached agreement in principle, but when I explained the proposed deal to the INP technical director, he rejected it outright. He wanted nothing to do with ILPES advisers, who in the past had "tried to run the institute."

Host governments could waive the secrecy of information clause in UN contracts if they insisted, but in Peru this required obtaining the approval of the National Security Council. Military officials inclined to stamp "confidential" even on toilet paper could hardly be expected to waive the secrecy clause in a technical assistance contract with a foreign organization. So our efforts to establish a longer-term technical assistance relationship with the INP came to a disappointing end. The only longer-term result of our Peruvian sojourn was that not only Florel but also her husband-to-be got hooked on Peru, later carried out research on their doctoral dissertations there, and subsequently published their work in books that won acclaim and helped them get positions as history professors in the same university (quite an achievement in view of anti-nepotism rules prevailing at the time).

CENTRAL AMERICAN RESIDENCE FUNDED BY USAID

Because of the failure of the Peruvian initiative, I needed to look for another foreign advisory assignment. The first thing that came up was again from the Ford Foundation, but not as a DAS adviser. The foundation offered me a position as resident representative in Santiago to help relocate abroad Chilean academics who had lost their jobs under the oppressive Pinochet dictatorship that seized power in 1973. Although the offer was very tempting, I had to take into account that our extended Chilean family could be placed in jeopardy from possible government reprisals on account of my work. After consultation with Nacha and careful reflection, we decided that the assignment would be too risky for her family and reluctantly turned it down.

At about the same time the DAS received a request for technical assistance from the Central American Institute of Business Administration (INCAE) located in Managua, Nicaragua. The ostensible purpose of the project, to be financed by USAID, was to help INCAE provide assistance to the Nicaraguan government for designing and implementing a program to reconstruct Managua after the devastating earthquake of the previous year that had turned the center of town into a pile of rubble. While visiting INCAE to evaluate the proposal I discovered that it also offered a much broader opportunity, one that I had been pursuing for some time. As a regional organization involved in research and outside consulting as well as teaching, INCAE had the potential to become a local partner of the DAS in providing technical assistance to other Latin American countries. This opportunity made the prospect of working with the Somoza dictatorship much less distasteful.

After completing my teaching and other ongoing commitments at Harvard, I moved to Nicaragua in 1974, this time by myself. Nacha had her own professional commitments in Framingham that she could not abandon at that time. So she spent a good part of her salary paying for monthly weekend trips to visit me in Managua until she was able to move down herself the following year. Leading a bachelor's life again before Nacha joined me was not easy, although Florel also flew down to keep me company for a while. She traveled with me on a couple of occasions to Guatemala and the Caribbean coast, on the latter trip in an old cargo plane to search for lost explorers in the jungle. Sweeping low over the trees was a thrilling experience, but more startling was the advice I was given when I complained that the cabin was too hot: "Just open the window!"

Soon after starting my work I came to realize that INCAE was not the kind of organization that would make an ideal local partner for the DAS in providing technical assistance to Latin American countries. The institute had been started with faculty assistance from the Harvard Business School and still had on the teaching staff a number of Americans who did not speak Spanish well. They taught their courses in English accompanied by an interpreter; even written examinations had to be translated for them to correct and grade! Most of the students, on the other hand, belonged to what was called the "Alfa Romeo set," sons of wealthy families who in many cases were unable to gain admittance to good universities abroad. Consistent with this elite image, the rector of the institute was an elegant man

Grandsons
clockwise from upper right:
Dennis, born May 17, 1978
Raji, born March 25, 1982
Alan, born October 11, 1975
Raffi, born January 16, 1985

who flew only first class when he traveled, and to my dismay once picked me up wearing white gloves in a chauffeured limousine to go fishing! Furthermore, most outside consulting by the teaching staff was carried out on an individual basis to supplement faculty salaries, not as part of INCAE's outreach program.

Personal security in Nicaragua also seemed rather tenuous, not so much from the smoking volcanoes that surrounded Managua and the frequent earthquakes (the only major earthquake we experienced in fact occurred on a trip to Lake Atitlan in Guatemala). The war between Sandinista guerrillas and government troops was beginning to heat up, and the maintenance of law and order showed signs of breaking down. Our house was broken into, so we hired a cowboy night watchman who turned out to be gun-happy, discharging his revolver at night to scare off alleged intruders. After his colleague next door shot off his finger playing with guns, I decided it was time for me to take direct responsibility for our security, which entailed spending a couple of tense hours one night persuading him to turn over his weapon. Public utility services were also unreliable, although we were able to keep supplied with water from the swimming pool in the back yard, which also served neighbors and the local cattle population in times of need.

Despite these disquieting conditions our small advisory group made progress in helping to build a public management program that began to attract students from government agencies. As INCAE's reputation in the field grew, the institute was also asked to conduct workshops and seminars for public officials in the region, including one for cabinet ministers in Costa Rica. But I was not satisfied with the meager growth in our outside consulting activities, especially our work with the Nicaraguan government on earthquake reconstruction. In Nicaragua, as in other mini-states where the power elite all know each other, most business seems to be conducted within networks of extended family and personal friends. Outsiders like us are not trusted, and for good reason as I eventually found out from our work in Managua. It became increasingly evident that a significant portion of earthquake reconstruction funds was being used to benefit Somoza's family and friends. This posed a serious dilemma for me: should I blow the whistle as a conscientious administrator of USAID money or go along with the scam?

When one of our short-term consultants came to Managua and said that he wanted to see his friend the U.S. ambassador, I decided that this was a good opportunity to raise the issue of corruption with him. I had also known the ambassador in Buenos Aires when he was a young USAID officer and used to go out with Nacha and me together with his Argentine girlfriend (whom he later married). At lunch in the embassy he greeted me with a surprised expression, saying "Dick! I didn't know you were working here; you've been below my radar." After listening quietly to my whistle-blowing, he said reassuringly that he would have to look into the matter. But since he never contacted me again and USAID continued its reconstruction assistance as usual, I suppose that I remained below his radar. Later

Live volcano near Managua, Nicaragua

it became clear that the priority of our embassy was to help fight the "Sandinista communist menace" at whatever cost.

My disenchantment with our project reached a peak a little later when the rector of INCAE called a meeting to discuss the institute's financial woes. As USAID funding dried up it was necessary to increase other revenue sources such as those from outside consulting. He said in effect that we were softies and should be more aggressive, as he had been as a lawyer, in charging clients as much as possible for as little work as possible. He rejected outright our strategy of using part of the consulting revenue to finance the preparation of public management teaching materials and the expansion of course offerings. It also did not help matters that my chief local counterpart, a bright academic economist who understood little about the practical consulting world, was at the time emotionally involved with his secretary, with whom he spent long periods closeted in his office each day while his advisers and staff tried unsuccessfully to communicate with him. So I recommended that our project with INCAE be terminated in 1976.

In contrast, Nacha's work in Nicaragua turned out to be much more satisfying. After arriving in Managua she soon became involved in orienting local U.S. Peace Corps volunteers, advising community development workers in low-income housing projects, and assisting day

*Alan on the
beach in
Costa Rica
with Mom
and Grandpa,
1976*

care centers sponsored by Mrs. Somoza, the president's wife. (Unlike
her husband, Mrs. Somoza seemed earnestly committed to improving the welfare of her constituents and later separated from the dictator.) We also were visited by Nanine with our first grandson, whom
we thoroughly enjoyed getting to know on a trip to the lovely beaches
of northern Costa Rica. So our stay in Central America had its satisfying moments.

In the longer term our project also contributed to changing the
image of INCAE after the fall of the Somoza dictatorship. I was able
to see first-hand what later happened to the institute when I was invited back a couple of times as a consultant to the Sandinista government by the new minister of trade, who had been a colleague at
INCAE by day and a Sandinista gun runner at night. Although the
main campus had been moved to Costa Rica, the facility in Managua
continued to function primarily as a center for training government
officials in public management. Eventually about half of INCAE's
students were enrolled in public management courses, thus in effect
changing the image of the institute as a country club for the "Alfa
Romeo set" to that of a more egalitarian institution (fortunately under new management) dedicated to improving the capacity of local
professionals to manage the development of their countries.

PROJECTS FINANCED WITH OIL MONEY

In the 1970s petroleum-exporting countries were enjoying immense windfall profits from the boom in oil prices. Two of these countries, Venezuela and Ecuador, turned to Harvard to ask for technical assistance that they were willing to fund themselves without foreign financial support. Upon returning from Central America I soon became involved in three of these projects.

The first two projects were in Venezuela, one with the Venezuelan Guayana Corporation (CVG) and the second with the Agrarian Credit Institute. The CVG was an official regional development corporation that had been allocated a big chunk of oil windfall profits to establish new industries, expand public utilities, and build a new city in the Orinoco River basin in the backward south of the country. Billions of dollars were being spent on construction of a large integrated steel mill and expansion in the production of iron ore and coal to supply the mill, on bauxite processing plants combined with large hydroelectric facilities to provide the power necessary to reduce the ore, and on development of forestry, oil sand deposits, and other natural resources and manufacturing facilities. The need for sound planning and coordination of such a vast program was obvious.

So before I returned to Harvard from Managua we agreed to provide technical assistance to the planning division of the CVG. Upon my return I became Cambridge backstopper of the project and made frequent trips to Venezuela. Our chief counterpart was an ethereal intellectual fascinated with computers and mathematical models who was well chosen to head a division that had utterly no influence in the real world of action. Since there were no serious financial constraints on carrying out CVG's investment program, the "dismal science" of economics (the optimal allocation of scarce resources among competing uses) was quite irrelevant. We therefore tried to concentrate our efforts on improving social and community development in Guayana, and Nacha was also contracted as a consultant to share her experience. But all studies and reports prepared by us and our counterparts ended up, so far as I know, in the files collecting dust.

I personally investigated and initiated the project with the Agrarian Credit Institute, a regional lending institution located in the semirural town of Barquisimeto in western Venezuela. The politically ambitious director of this institute was bent on promoting more diversified development of the area. In principle his ambition made a good deal of sense: this was the time when the concept of "integrated rural development" was very popular, and the region was abundantly endowed with resources. So we proceeded to contract a pair of junior resident advisers (no senior experts were willing to take up residence in the rather remote place) and to supplement our assistance with frequent visits by more senior personnel. Almost from the start the director showed displeasure with our recruitment. It turned out that he was not as interested in the quality of our work as in the prestige of rubbing elbows with well-known Harvard luminaries to promote his political career.

So both Venezuelan projects terminated with a profound sense of disillusionment. Obviously we and our counterparts did not share the same objectives of institution building and training for practical policy planning and analysis from the very beginning. Upon further reflection it occurs to me that such objectives are probably unrealistic in institutions flush with money that are not under pressure to make decisions about policy tradeoffs. Neither institution we worked with was under this kind of pressure in the conditions then prevailing in Venezuela. These conditions are aptly described by Isabel Allende in her autobiographical book *Paula*: "…a hot and anarchic country languishing in the petroleum bonanza, a Saudi society where waste reached absurd limits; even bread and eggs were imported from Miami because it was more comfortable to do so than to produce them" (free translation from the Spanish edition, pp. 163-64).

The proposed project in Ecuador was more serious, but it also reflected exuberant expectations of almost unlimited funding from the oil bonanza. The national petroleum corporation wanted to use part of its windfall earnings to carry out a comprehensive development program in Santa Elena, a semi-arid peninsula jutting out into the Pacific Ocean where off-shore oil had been found and a large new petroleum refinery was to be built. The proposed program not only embraced large-scale expansion of infrastructure facilities (transportation, water supply, electric power, etc.) and non-agricultural employment opportunities but also projects to protect the environment, improve housing and social conditions, and preserve ancient cultural sites. The program even included creation of a science museum patterned on the one in Boston!

Needless to say, this was a very exciting project for an organization like ours that prided itself in being multidisciplinary. So I led an evaluation mission composed of a couple of Harvard faculty members to investigate the proposal. We were well impressed with the possibilities and were prepared to start negotiating an advisory contract. At this very moment, however, the price of oil collapsed and the project had to be abandoned as the developing world during the 1980s entered into the gravest international debt crisis since the Great Depression. But I am getting ahead of events that had been occurring back home.

CHAPTER VIII ∾
NEW RULES OF THE GAME

*T*he DAS had fallen on hard times at the beginning of the 1970s. My colleagues were having just as much trouble in the rest of the world filling the gap left by the Ford Foundation as I was having in Latin America. New funders, agendas, and good projects turned out to be very hard to come by. Our overall budget was in deficit, and questions raised in the Dorfman Report about the relevance of the DAS to Harvard teaching and research remained unanswered.

Just at the moment when the very survival of the DAS seemed threatened, Harvard's recently appointed president, Derek Bok, came to our rescue. Partly influenced perhaps by his wife, daughter of a renowned Swedish scholar in the field of international development, the president strongly reaffirmed the University's public service commitment to poor countries; and in 1974 he reorganized the DAS into the Harvard Institute for International Development (HIID). This reorganization strengthened our ties to professional schools at the University, especially in the fields of education, public health, law, and eventually the Kennedy School of Government.

HIID thus became a better reflection of the multidisciplinary character of the University than was the DAS, whose ties had been primarily with the economics department. The change also facilitated a shift in emphasis away from providing national policy planning and analysis agencies with technical assistance, the demand for which was declining. HIID thus became better positioned to satisfy the growing needs of developing countries in a broader array of sectors and specialized subjects.

Every important change, however, has its downside. HIID began to reflect not only the multidisciplinary character of the University but also its disciplinary compartmentalization. The DAS was a more compact, homogeneous, and collegial organization of professionals who shared common backgrounds and experience. Originally we occupied only a few offices and spoke to each other almost daily. HIID became a much larger, diverse, and compartmentalized group of professionals who often did not speak the same language and found it extremely difficult to collaborate in truly *inter*disciplinary work, just like most university professors.

Harvard University also follows a policy of "each tub on its own bottom." This policy requires that each school or department of the University (HIID was now treated like a school) be self-financing – each one should generate enough income over time to cover salaries and benefits as well as a proper share of overhead costs. Such a policy is of course understandable, indeed necessary, for any institution or business that doesn't receive outside subsidies. Public service activities of such organizations are, however, often cross-subsidized from general revenue, but HIID was not explicitly given this kind of assistance. The institute's status as a public service provider therefore remained in doubt.

During the heyday of the DAS we didn't have to scramble for money – the Ford Foundation and other agencies and developing country governments asked us to carry out more projects than we could handle. We were therefore able to be selective, to insist on certain conditions, and to reject or withdraw from projects that we did not like. When back at the University after overseas assignments, we also didn't feel under any pressure to cover the cost of translating our experience into teaching and research. The policy of "every tub on its own bottom" in a more competitive technical assistance environment changed the previous rules of the game: it now became more difficult to be selective in choosing or discontinuing projects, and unfunded teaching and research had to be squeezed out of our spare time. I almost felt that I was back at INCAE.

Finally, the new environment was less hospitable to generalists like myself. The growing demand for technical assistance was for specialized expertise, not only in specific sectors or on specific topics but increasingly in high-tech areas such as training in computer skills and the design and application of mathematical models. Developing country governments and international funding agencies thus began to place more emphasis on recruiting high-tech experts, especially "heavyweights" with an international reputation in their specialized fields.

In response to these changes I decided that I had to develop a new area of specialization. I chose the subject of state-owned enterprises (SOEs) in developing countries. Such enterprises had expanded rapidly in recent years. In many countries they were responsible for operating most public utilities and they dominated important industries such as mining and petroleum. In numerous cases, however, SOEs were becoming a drag on development: the services they provided were often poor; they were unable to satisfy growing demand; and some of them were generating large deficits that threatened to destabilize entire economies.

The ideological solution to these problems is privatization, but I was convinced that the root causes run much deeper than government ownership *per se*. Privatization can of course help provide access to investment capital, new technology, and modern managerial know-how, but large SOEs can usually buy these things if they really want to and if governments let them. The root cause of poor SOE performance is not lack of availability of capital, technology, and know-how but inefficient utilization. Efficiency depends on motivation. Very few managers, either public or private, will knock themselves out to maximize efficiency unless they are pressured to do so and are rewarded accordingly – it is only human to want to be liked and to enjoy life. But good guys seldom win if they have to fight for survival in a fiercely competitive world with no freebies from the boss. I should know – I've always enjoyed enough freebies to be a good guy.

"Fiercely competitive" is certainly not an accurate description of the world in which public utilities and important industries operate in most developing countries. These enterprises, both public and private, tend to be highly politicized by measures to protect them from free-market competition: prices fixed at artificial levels, corporate welfare (i.e., indiscriminate fiscal subsidies), cheap credit, nepotism, outside intervention in labor relations, imposition of social obligations without compensation, government bailouts of bankrupt firms, etc. Not even in the United States, a bastion of private enterprise, can one seriously claim that public utilities and large private businesses are free from this kind of politicization. Imagine what can go on in smaller poor countries when underpaid public officials deal with powerful public and private business leaders and politicized labor unions!

So in 1973, just after my return from Peru, I organized a six-week public enterprise workshop (PEW) to discuss these issues with SOE managers, government officials, and interested professionals from developing countries and international organizations. The PEW was the first workshop organized by HIID and soon became financially self-sustaining, continuing to be held at Harvard every summer up to the present time. Getting it started, however, was a real tour de force. We thought we understood the main problems and issues concerning SOEs, but we had almost no practical experience working with them in the field, and precious little literature had been published on the subject up to that time. I therefore thought it necessary to run the workshop like a discussion group so that we could learn from the participants as much as they learned from us.

It was difficult to get the ball rolling at the beginning of each session because most participants were accustomed to hearing classroom lectures and were reluctant to speak out frankly, but eventually they would get into the swim and then it would be hard to get some of them (often the least relevant ones) to give others a chance to talk. We were constantly challenged to overcome differences in language, religious practices, eating habits, and the like; and considerable delicacy was required to resolve problems created by senior officials who were accustomed to being waited on hand and foot and sometimes expected local service staff to make themselves available for recreational purposes. But most participants seemed satisfied with their experience and recommended the workshop to colleagues when they got back home, and the teaching staff certainly learned a great deal.

This learning process could be cumulative, however, only if the turnover of workshop teaching staff was kept to a minimum. I soon discovered, though, that only one or two Harvard colleagues were willing or able to make a longer-term commitment to workshop teaching, so I had to turn elsewhere to build a multidisciplinary team. Upon return from my overseas assignment at INCAE I therefore organized the Boston Area Public Enterprise Group (BAPEG), which was composed chiefly of professors from nearby universities. Since we needed funds to build up a specialized library, prepare additional teaching materials, invite outside experts to attend BAPEG-sponsored seminars and conferences, and launch a newsletter, I approached the Ford Foundation for seed money. The foundation was again forthcoming, so BAPEG took off in a flurry of activity. So far so good, but this early success did not enable me to become a heavyweight in my new field of expertise.

Even if I had had the temperament and ability to become a "heavyweight," I don't think it would have been possible at Harvard. State-owned enterprise was a topic that did not fit into any scholarly disci-

Egypt, 1992

pline; no school or department wanted to include the subject in its regular curriculum. The head of the economics department at another local university, however, invited me to offer public enterprise as a joint special field in economics and business in his PhD program. Still unwilling to resign from HIID, I recommended a bright young economist, Leroy Jones, who taught with me in the PEW. He accepted the job and went on to develop a first-rate curriculum with a high-tech flourish. He constructed a computer model to measure the performance of SOEs that attracted international attention; he also copyrighted it for use in his own off-campus consulting firm.

His reputation grew as I found it necessary to delegate increasing responsibility to him for running BAPEG. I simply didn't have the time because I was on airplanes flying to distant places – such as the trips to Venezuela and Nicaragua mentioned in the last chapter – on various consulting assignments for HIID. What bothered me most about being a frequent flyer was not so much losing control of BAPEG as being away from my family. There was an element of danger too, especially commuting around places like Africa when the weather is bad.

I remember one incident in particular on a shuttle flight from Dakar to Banjul in West Africa. Shortly after takeoff we ran into the most violent storm I ever experienced in the sky. Things started flying around the cabin and people were screaming, but the crew didn't say a word for more than an hour until a voice finally came over the intercom, "prepare for landing." We had managed to return to Dakar.

Upon boarding the plane next morning to make another try, a native market lady dressed in turban and flowing gown came up to me and asked, "may I sit next to you." She had been on the harrowing flight the night before, so this time she clutched my hand during the whole half hour trip to Banjul.

I was also traveling abroad to organize workshops overseas similar to the PEW. My idea was that local workshops would be less expensive and would attract a larger number of participants from the same country who could create a critical mass of advocates for reform. I thought that the ideas we were trying to disseminate through the PEW and BAPEG would have a better chance of taking root if we could also find local collaborators who would help prepare teaching materials. People learn better when course content is specifically related to their own experience.

Obtaining effective local collaboration in running public enterprise workshops overseas was not easy. In the Dominican Republic in 1987 a local university agreed to join us in sponsoring a week-long event funded by USAID that was attended by the vice president and other high officials of the country. But we could not find a qualified colleague to help us prepare and teach a case on the Dominican sugar corporation; we had to do it ourselves. Similarly, even though the joint Egyptian-American Fulbright Association was eager to support local collaboration in organizing a workshop in Cairo, the teaching case prepared by our counterpart turned out to be unusable. In the absence of any teaching material directly related to the personal experience of participants, I suspect that what they most remembered later about the workshop was the earthquake that shook the building violently and emptied the classroom.

Nacha was terrified too by the Cairo earthquake, which was televised dramatically by CNN in Geneva, where she was visiting her sister. Despite my reassurances over the phone when she finally got through, Nacha was not convinced that I was still in one piece until she later joined me in Egypt on a majestic boat trip down the Nile and a tour of the island of Rhodes. She herself was in fact in greater potential danger at this time than I was. She was working, often until after dark, on Hispanic community development, bilingual education, and child care for poor families in the South End of Boston, Roxbury, and other communities afflicted by racial tensions. She carried Mace but never had occasion to use it because the word was passed around that she should not be molested.

In the late 1970s and early 1980s, Nacha also had been able to join me on a few other trips abroad to Malaysia, Sri Lanka, Kenya, Uganda, and The Gambia. The highlights were in Sri Lanka after a rough boat excursion to an outer coral island in nearby Maldives, a haven for snorkeling and nude bathing. We were also lucky to be able to go on a wild animal safari in Kenya, where the animals wander free while people watch them from inside their four-wheel-drive cages. But my consulting assignments on these trips were not very successful. I failed to organize support for conducting local workshops, and my advice on how to improve public enterprise performance seemed to fall on deaf ears.

I was trying to persuade my counterparts that the best way to improve SOE performance was to free managers from excessive bureaucratic controls that foster politicization – that governments should maintain an "arm's length" relationship with their enterprises so that managers had enough operational autonomy to be held accountable for results. It would then be possible to motivate managers by rewarding or penalizing them based on their performance, as is done in most successful business firms, both private and public.

The Malaysian government, however, was determined to improve SOE performance through strengthening central government monitoring by means of a computerized information system. In Sri Lanka my chief government counterpart was convinced that the job could be done by a parliamentary audit committee, despite evidence to the contrary brought to light in my work with a local research institute. His response was to cancel my consultancy. In Kenya, Uganda and later Somalia I was not even able to get a project started. Few officials seemed willing to reduce government interference so as to allow managers to behave more like businessmen than politicians.

My continuing effort to organize public enterprise workshops overseas with effective local collaboration, however, was finally rewarded in an unlikely place: The Gambia in West Africa. The Gambia doesn't have a local university or research institute like the Dominican Republic or Egypt, but I met some talented people while working as a public enterprise consultant to the government. A few of them came to the PEW in Cambridge for training and later collaborated in preparing materials and teaching in the workshop we organized there. Direct local involvement was greatly appreciated by sponsors and participants alike. I remember receiving a visit at my hotel by one of my chief counterparts in the agency I was working with. He was very

Public Enterprise Workshop in The Gambia, 1988

pleased with the workshop and wanted to consolidate our working relationship, but this was not to be.

My consulting assignment in The Gambia was to help the government design and implement SOE performance contracts. The purpose of these contracts was precisely what I had been pressing for: to negotiate reciprocal obligations between government and SOEs that allowed public enterprise performance to be measured by results. My counterparts and I learned a great deal, for example that the largest SOE, the produce marketing board, no longer served any useful purpose and should be liquidated. But conditions were not favorable for taking this kind of action or for introducing performance contracts. The country was very short of good managerial talent, and enterprises were not obliged to provide the information necessary for monitoring performance. Perhaps the most serious obstacle was that The Gambia was another mini-state like Nicaragua where most transactions seem to be conducted within networks of extended family and personal friends – politicization was a part of daily life. So performance contracts were never put to a fair test, and my consultancy ended when the project funder, USAID, decided that all SOEs had to be privatized.

Another opportunity to test SOE performance contracts soon presented itself when I was asked by the Bolivian government, on the recommendation of Leroy Jones, to help improve their public enterprises. This test held promise of being fairer than it had been in The Gambia: good managerial talent was not so scarce in Bolivia, enterprises were obliged to provide the information necessary to monitor performance, and most transactions were not carried out within intimate personal networks. But first I had to sell the idea to my new counterparts.

So in 1989 I set out for La Paz to organize the new project, which was financed by the Inter-American Development Bank. I had been there more than thirty years earlier when I worked for ECLA, but then I was a young man not fazed by the two-mile altitude. This time was quite different. Shortly after leaving the airport and descending the precipice into the city I experienced the shortness of breath, headaches, and later the sleeplessness at night that most visitors complain of. "Drink lots of coca tea" (an infusion of leaves from the coca plant in hot water) is the customary advice, but I found that the only effective remedy was to spend one or two weeks building up my red blood corpuscle count. I never found a remedy, however, for keeping my pipe lit.

Selling the idea of performance contracts in Bolivia was not difficult. The deputy head of the ministry I was assigned to had attended the PEW several years earlier, and the situation in the country was quite conducive. Public enterprises suffered from the familiar malaise of excess manpower, uneven service, imposition of social obligations without compensation, etc., with one important exception: they did not represent a significant drain on the government treasury. Government had imposed stringent financial controls, even requiring SOEs to obtain prior approval before writing checks on their own bank accounts. These controls naturally disrupted the normal conduct of business, delaying the procurement of materials and equipment, causing a pile-up of unpaid bills, and motivating SOE managers to secrete funds in hidden places.

Both the government and SOE managers were therefore predisposed in principle to negotiate reciprocal obligations under which government would relax financial controls in exchange for targeted improvements in SOE performance. The first step was to examine the internal organization, management information systems, cost structures, and markets for each of the major SOEs to identify the changes needed to make them more efficient. For this purpose we recruited a group of internationally recognized experts in each line of business. They were a fascinating group of characters who provided all of us, on both the government and enterprise sides, with a stimulating learning experience. One of them came with a huge laptop computer, containing a large database on petroleum company operations around the world, which he always carried with him. I thought he would pass out one day when the elevators were out of service and he had to climb fourteen flights of stairs to a meeting.

The next step was to negotiate reciprocal obligations in the contracts. This was a new experience for government officials and SOE managers alike. Government was accustomed to *imposing* obligations on enterprises, which then tried to wriggle out of them by wheeling and dealing behind the scenes. The fundamental idea of performance contracts was to motivate both parties to comply voluntarily with their obligations. If they did so, then SOE managers would receive a share of reduced costs or increased profits as bonuses, and government officials could claim credit for improving public enterprise performance. But some contract terms were very difficult to negotiate. The railway would have to sell some property to finance separation payments to redundant workers; the telecommunications enterprise would have to accept greater competition in exchange for less government regulation; and government would have to compensate the electric power company for revenue lost if prices were fixed at artificially low levels, etc.

Compensation of enterprise social obligations was one of the thorniest issues to negotiate, because each side wanted the other to bear the burden. The pressure to improve the lot of the poor and of those living in remote areas cannot be avoided in Bolivia. A large part of the population subsists below the poverty line, as is evident from the squalor of Indian mothers with scrawny babies begging on the streets of La Paz and from the dearth of public services in most communities outside of the main cities. The trip from La Paz to the Yungas is thrilling for people like us who marvel at the rapidly changing landscape of snow-capped peaks, waterfalls, precipices, and tropical jungle over a distance of only 50 miles; but for local people it must be hell to bounce along in rickety vehicles on dangerously steep dirt roads often gutted by rockslides.

Despite the poverty and deficient public services, life in Bolivia was not a dreary experience fraught with danger at every turn, as Nacha can testify. She joined me several times on my consulting trips to La Paz, where we installed ourselves in a housekeeping apartment in a modest hotel. Almost everybody was very friendly and remarkably

Nacha and Dick at Lake Titicaca, Bolivia, 1991

honest. When I once left my camera by mistake in a nearby restaurant over night, it was there the next day safely put away; and when I lost a credit card from my wallet on a downtown street, someone picked it up and came running after me to return it. Even though we frequently visited congested street markets on weekends to inspect local handicraft and exotic items for sale like llama fetuses (a good luck charm), only once did Nacha have her purse slit in the local smugglers market picturesquely named "Little Miami" (Miamicito). Almost everybody seemed to enjoy and participate in the frequent processions and carnivals celebrated on city streets, even the president himself who we watched descend from his grandstand seat to join dancers in the famous annual carnival in Oruro.

A number of performance contracts were successfully negotiated with major public enterprises. The first was with the electricity corporation, which exceeded its targets and received a substantial bonus. It attracted so much attention that the World Bank organized a special seminar in Washington to discuss the case, which was presented by one of my chief local counterparts who was later hired by the Bank as a member of its professional staff. But the system of performance contracts did not solve the problem of politicization. My young counterparts were no match for seasoned SOE managers who tried to impede verification of contract compliance, and the staff of

Dance procession on the main street of La Paz, Bolivia

sectoral ministries felt threatened by the new system. Success of the project depended on the forceful support of our minister, who unfortunately was losing his battle for survival. He was soon replaced by a much more conservative businessman who declared that performance contracts were an obstacle to privatization.

So our project came to an end, despite the fact that SOE performance contracts actually facilitated subsequent privatization. SOEs that began restructuring to fulfill contract obligations to compete more effectively in competitive markets were attractive to private investors, and quantification of the costs and benefits of subsidizing SOE social obligations helped improve government regulation of privatized public utilities. But the most important personal impact of this experience was the realization that I had become a full-fledged new missionary seeking to reform the developing world.

CHAPTER IX ∼
PROMOTING POLICY REFORM

*I*n 1980 the director of HIID could still say, "We try to get our people to be like the ideal civil servant who helps the decision-maker identify his problems and outline alternatives but leaves him to choose according to his objectives." This statement now seems rather quaint both in terms of the presumed gender of the "decision-maker" as well as the description of what macroeconomic advisers are expected to do. The tide of missionary zeal for using technical assistance primarily to promote private enterprise and open markets had in fact already begun to swell well before 1980.

A prominent example of the zealous missionary was Professor Harberger of the University of Chicago, a firm believer in orthodox free market economics, who became chief foreign adviser to Chile when Pinochet seized power. His brand of "shock therapy" for sick countries has been described as surgery without anesthesia – slash government expenditures, cut monetary expansion, and remove free-market obstructions quickly without regard for the patient's discomfort. Harberger's advice was accepted not only in Chile but also in other Latin American countries where his ex-students, known as the "Chicago Boys," reached positions of authority in conservative military regimes during the 1970s.

The tide of free market reform was reinforced by the so-called Asian Miracle, the phenomenal success of several East Asian countries nicknamed "tigers" or "dragons." Unlike the "lambs" of South Asia, Africa, and most of Latin America, the dragons were fiercely competitive in promoting export-led growth (albeit with more government intervention than the Chicago Boys would approve of). The attractiveness of this growth strategy was enhanced by the international debt crisis that swept the developing world beginning in 1982. Country after country found it necessary to undergo shock therapy, downsizing their governments and imposing strict austerity to divert foreign exchange to debt payments. They had no choice other than to become new dragons or pariahs in the world community. Foreign creditors and international financial agencies refused to grant relief unless debtor countries accepted open market reforms.

Despite the high human cost of the reforms – rising unemployment, falling standards of living for most people, shrinking government expenditures on social programs, and often brutal repression of opposition groups – the "lost decade" of the 1980s did have at least one redeeming feature. Quite a few poor countries abandoned their naive populist faith that they could grow successfully while depending on export revenue from one or two primary commodities and on the dynamic expansion of isolated domestic markets. Globalization of the world economy was becoming a painful reality.

The advance of reformist zeal in technical assistance nevertheless encountered some resistance. The appointment of Professor Harberger to become the new director of HIID in 1980 created a huge stir at Harvard. Student protests and public debates focused mainly on Harberger's involvement with Pinochet and other dictators in Latin America, but my own opposition to his appointment was motivated by his high profile, activist style and by his apparent neglect of human and institutional constraints on policy reform. In a private meeting with colleagues, for example, I asked him how he would use a non-economic adviser in an overseas project. He thought for a moment and then responded, "I would ask him to interview grandmothers on how much better off their children and grandchildren are than they were when they grew up."

I had known Harberger for years and had the greatest respect for his brilliance as an economist, but I thought that his drawbacks would be lethal as director of HIID. He clearly could think of no substantive role for non-economists in policy analysis. I therefore joined with a few other, mostly non-economist, HIID fellows in a meeting with Harvard's president Bok to lobby against his appointment. Our vocal opposition may have had something to do with his later refusal to accept appointment as director of HIID.

International resistance to direct foreign intervention in policy making was led by the United Nations, the membership of which was dominated by developing countries. At their urging the U.N. General Assembly adopted in 1974 a resolution establishing the New International Economic Order to "correct inequalities and redress any existing injustices." During the 1980s aid recipients also began to raise questions about the share of development assistance funds supporting foreign experts, especially in Africa, where support for some

100,000 experts absorbed over half of aid funds. One official even described the use of expatriate resident technical assistance by aid donors as "a systematic destructive force which is undermining the development of capacity in Africa." The response of the United Nations was to shift increasing responsibility for designing technical assistance programs to recipient countries themselves.

Most other aid donors, however, continued to exert high-profile pressure for reform. I will never forget my experience with USAID in Paraguay in 1990. I accepted an invitation to help the new Paraguayan regime, elected to replace the longest surviving dictator in Latin America, to strengthen its national policy analysis and planning agency. When I arrived at the airport in Asunción, I was appalled to be whisked off by USAID officials to accompany the U.S. ambassador in a meeting with the new president. We were of course accompanied by a bevy of news reporters and photographers, who later pursued me incessantly asking for an interview. At the insistence of one of my Paraguayan counterparts, I finally consented to speak to one of his reporter friends. The next day his newspaper carried the front page headline, "Mallon believes that Paraguayan economic policy is no good." That of course spelled the end of my effort to help provide in-service training for local technocrats.

My first (and last) residence abroad as a full-fledged reformist missionary was in Bangladesh, where from 1983 to 1987 I headed a HIID project to reform trade and industrial policy (TIP). The TIP project was funded by the International Development Association, the "soft money" lending window of the World Bank. The bank was pressuring Bangladesh to open up its economy and wanted us to help policy makers adopt a development strategy similar to that of the East Asian dragons. Such a strategy made a good deal of sense for Bangladesh. The country was in very bad shape: more than half its imports were financed by foreign aid because its main export commodity (jute) was in decline, and protected manufacturing industries were so inefficient that they could not compete in international markets. Its most important source of foreign exchange earnings was from exports of people who remitted part of their earnings back home.

There is no denying that Bangladesh has an export surplus of people, more than 100,000,000 of them living in an area smaller than the state of Wisconsin. And during the monsoon season a large part of this area is under water, so that inhabitants have to scramble to higher ground and compete with snakes and other critters for space.

The monsoon floods are also a boon: the massive flow of silt from the Himalayas renews the fertility of the soil and creates new islands in the Bay of Bengal. Bangladesh is one of the few countries in the world with a growing geographical area. But the opportunity of moving to the new islands is a mixed blessing for land-starved peasants, many of whom are swept away every few years by mighty cyclones that engulf the bay.

Bangladesh is a country of shocking extremes – misery and joy, violence and artistry, squalor and beauty. Beggars constitute such an important part of the labor force that they are recognized as a legitimate profession in the national census and have their own representative in parliament. Born in 1972 after a bloody civil war in which many university intellectuals were systematically slaughtered, the country has never had a chief of state who finished his or her term of office without being assassinated, jailed, or overthrown. Labor disputes are often settled by *hartals*, during which workers hold their bosses hostage until they give in or police take over by force. Cholera, malaria, and other life-threatening diseases are endemic in the clammy climate. Despite the hurt and discomfort, however, most people manage to retain a poetic dignity, and the ravaged land still glows in magnificent sunsets reflected in peaceful ponds surrounded by lush vegetation.

So off I went in the spring of 1983 to organize the project and set up a new home alone. Nacha had to complete work commitments in Boston and, even more important for our family, accompany our daughter Nanine while she had major surgery. As in Pakistan a quarter of a century earlier, I found it necessary to recruit a full staff of servants in our new quarters. The staff didn't last very long after Nacha finally joined me, especially when she found them taking their siestas under the dining room table to keep cool on the tiled floor. She nevertheless had to compromise some of her standards. She hired a Buddhist *hamal* (assistant to the head bearer) who was not permitted by his religion to kill any living thing, so when biting ants invaded the house she reluctantly allowed him to keep sweeping them out through the windows.

The project I directed was a large one with a dozen resident advisers and numerous consultants. It was headquartered in the national Planning Commission, the grounds of which were littered with rusting vehicles and other equipment inherited from previous technical assistance projects. Even more disconcerting, I discovered that the seven different units we were supposed to advise were scattered over four different government agencies, each with its own agenda and control over its share of the TIP budget. Coordination of this patchwork quilt was assigned to a high-level committee that could seldom meet for lack of a quorum.

The organizational nightmare reminded me a bit of the *Rocket*, the paddlewheel steamer that provided "express service" from Dhaka to the southwestern port of Khulna. When I took the trip early on in my residence to familiarize myself with the country, the boat meandered through the delta without any particular schedule. It stopped frequently at intermediate ports, where people hurrying to get off charged into a phalanx of people rushing to get on, jostling each other on two flimsy boards that served as a gangplank. Most passengers traveled in steerage on the floor of the engine room, where they slept helter-skelter among their bundles; and children ran freely among moving parts of the machinery, which must have been manufactured prior to World War I and provided little protection against accidents.

Our disorganized project was similarly prone to mishaps, so I tried to appeal to one of our senior Bangladeshi friends for help. His answer was, "it takes two to tango." In other words, no senior civil servant could tell a colleague in another department what to do. So I selected as my tango partner the head of one of the key agencies we advised, the Tariff Commission. The chairman of the Commission was a retired admiral who ruled with a naval discipline unsuited to the development of a professional staff organization. What a dance we had! We started off frequently stepping on each other's toes, especially when one of our own advisers, an Afghani economist, sided with the admiral against the project team. There was nothing I could do but get in step with the admiral while trying to teach him a more effective leadership style.

Fortunately, getting to know the admiral and his charming wife was a surprisingly agreeable experience. I shared his interest in collecting orchids, became an active member of his charity organization, and accompanied him on occasional trips. The trip we took with our wives to his home village was especially memorable. After a rough drive on dirt roads, we boarded a country boat to continue our journey. The boat was about the size of a large canoe with hard wooden benches and no protection against the searing sun. A little man dressed in turban and loin cloth poled it with increasing difficulty through canals choked with water lilies, which I pulled aside

Nacha with school children and their mothers in a Bangladesh village, 1986

while sitting on the prow soaked in sweat. Nacha became the special attraction when we reached the village. She was seated like a queen on a throne surrounded by local women and fanned with a large palm frond to keep her cool.

Nacha always attracted attention wherever she went. While setting up a day-care center for children of women working in an embroidery factory, she took the kids to a nearby zoo and found herself surrounded by curious onlookers; she felt that she should be in a cage instead of the animals. When we once visited the beach at Cox's Bazaar dressed in bathing suits (Muslim women never wear them), we suddenly found ourselves surrounded by a hundred men who had to be dispersed by the police. Nacha also astounded the local populace when she later road astride on the back of a motorcycle to visit villages where she was helping to introduce an improved curriculum for primary schools.

Luckily, I didn't attract anything like the same attention. My main difficulty with people was that our local counterparts (with a few prominent exceptions) lacked the professional qualifications necessary to take advantage of the intensive in-service training programs we organized. Most of them were poorly paid, bureaucratic paper pushers who were at a complete loss when placed before a computer to calculate the effective rate of protection of a domestic industry. We therefore had to turn to Bangladeshi universities and research institutes to recruit local consultants to work with us. This turned out to be an advantage for the project.

Many local intellectuals still identified with the government's command and control ideology embraced by the socialist People's Republic of Bangladesh when it was founded. If new policies designed to reduce the country's dependence on foreign charity and falling jute exports were to gain broad support, it would first be necessary to convince intellectual leaders that existing policies were counter-productive. The best way to do this would be to invite them to collaborate in our research. But many of them were reluctant to join the project, as I learned when I tried to recruit my Bangladeshi "son" as a local consultant.

My proxy son was the little boy I had taught to play chess at the home of my former counterpart in Pakistan more than twenty years earlier. I had tracked him all the way up through his study for a PhD in economics at Stanford University, from which he had recently returned to work in the oldest and most prestigious research institute in Bangladesh. The institute was directed by a prominent member of the national socialist Awami League party who had distrusted foreign advisers since the days of the Harvard Group in Pakistan. So my Bangladeshi son was never able to work with us, although we later engaged him and his institute colleagues in active debate in the seminars we organized to discuss the results of our studies.

In view of initial widespread opposition to the reformist agenda of TIP's terms of reference, not only from intellectuals but even more from government bureaucrats whose power depended on pervasive state intervention in the economy, we decided to follow an educational strategy. Rather than preach hell-fire to policy makers who refused conversion to the faith of economic liberalism, we tried to iden-

Nacha raring to take off on a visit to a Bangladesh village, 1986

93

tify policy flaws that no serious economist could justify regardless of his or her ideology. The most glaring flaw was the irrational structure of protection. Tariffs ranging from zero to over 100 percent were charged indiscriminately on imports of final goods, intermediate products, and raw materials, with the result that the effective rate of protection of domestic industries varied between negative and infinite. The structure of protection was so erratic that it even allowed industries to survive that generated negative value-added.

Florel with Steve, married August 1978

Another reform we thought would not face serious opposition was to provide incentives for increasing the domestic value-added in exports. For example, garment exports were expanding rapidly at this time, but they generated minimal net foreign exchange earnings because almost all inputs (cloth, buttons, zippers, packing materials, etc.) were imported duty free into bonded warehouses. Why not give domestic producers of these inputs a chance to compete with imports, we asked. This could be done by compensating domestic producers for the tariffs and taxes they paid that artificially raised their costs. A great idea, our counterparts agreed, but implementation of the incentive system would be very complicated. What they really meant was that bureaucrats responsible for calculating and paying appropriate compensation would undermine incentives by trying to extort bribes.

Corruption was indeed endemic in Bangladesh, as it is in most countries where public officials are poorly paid and have broad administrative discretion to interpret the law. I will never forget Nacha's experience when she went to the central post office in Dhaka to claim a package received from our daughters containing family photos. She

Young professional mothers can still laugh, 1986

was given the runaround for two days by clerks expecting *bhakshish* until she marched into a director's office and demanded the package. Similarly, we once had to use the full borrowing limits of our personal credit cards to finance project expenditures because disbursement of local currency funds was blocked by avaricious bureaucrats. I finally phoned the comptroller general of the country to complain, and within a few hours disbursements began to flow again.

It was obvious that our project had to address the problem of corruption directly in our policy studies and recommendations. Instead of pontificating about the evils of corruption, we decided to take a more realistic approach. To reduce delays and give domestic producers of inputs for exporters greater leverage in bargaining for *bhakshish*, we advocated adoption of parallel incentive systems. Different government agencies would then have to compete with each other for clients. This approach might be called the marketization of corruption, which in a command and control economy is not all bad. Each individual enterprise that succeeded in obtaining a license to go into business, for example, received a "passbook" that detailed the type and quantity of items it could import. The clandestine resale of passbook permits made import controls more flexible and enabled a vibrant industrial complex of unlicensed firms to develop across the river from Dhaka.

We were always looking for windows of opportunity to mobilize support for reform instead of attacking the opposition head on. The growing ship-breaking industry provided such an opportunity. It was an ideal industry for a cheap-labor country like Bangladesh: workers armed with sledge hammers and acetylene torches swarmed

A near miss near Dhaka

over old, beached vessels, cutting up scrap to use in steel re-rolling mills. The main obstacle to expansion of ship-breaking was the monopoly enjoyed by the state-owned steel mill that restricted re-rolling mills from competing in the manufacture and sale of certain steel products. The victims of the monopoly, both re-rollers and consumers, proved to be much more vocal than supporters of restrictions when we raised the issue with policy makers.

Reforms thus advanced gradually but with more stress than I had ever experienced before. The stress came in part from violent events, such as the tornado funnel that touched ground within a mile of where I was standing in an open field by the river. I also got caught in a protest demonstration while driving my jeep home from work one afternoon and almost had to run over a protester to escape the mob. Driving through the chaotic traffic of rickshaws, people and animals, sometimes in flooded streets with water reaching the floorboards, was no fun either. But most of the stress came from the struggle to prevent counterpart agencies from diverting the project to promote their own agendas.

Perhaps the most serious threat to the project came when the admiral retired as chairman of the Tariff Commission. He had become one of our strongest supporters and even joined our training classes to learn to use computers. His replacement, however, was an autocratic civil servant who wanted to take over the project with the assistance of our Afghani colleague. After a few months of disagreeable confrontations, he also was replaced as chairman by the father of one of our consultants. The new chairman not only began to collaborate with us closely but also took the initiative to introduce a series of reforms based on TIP studies.

The most important impact of the more than a hundred studies we published was, in my opinion, not so much the specific reforms they inspired at the time – it was the perceptible change in the way trade and industry policy was discussed in Bangladesh. Arguments pro and con began to raise legitimate issues instead of simply bogging down in ideological rhetoric. Debate in the numerous seminars and conferences we organized became better informed. Trade associations began to collect statistics and to prepare their own studies. It was even possible to discuss openly with civil servants the role of corruption (which we called "side payments") in the implementation of trade and industrial policies.

By the time our resident advisory mission came to an end in mid-1986, I was therefore reasonably satisfied that our project had made a difference. But Nacha and I could hardly wait to go back home, not only to see our daughters again but also to avoid becoming hardened to the sight of abject poverty. To maintain our own sanity we were no longer seeing the suffering all around us. Despite our surfeit of suffering and my commitment to return to Bangladesh several times again during the following year to complete project work, we couldn't resist the temptation to travel home via China, another very poor country. Fascinating changes were beginning to take place there, and tourists from the People's Republic of Bangladesh received steep price discounts from the official Chinese tourist agency.

After arriving in Guangzhou (formerly Canton) by train from Hong Kong, we waited for our tour guide on the platform until it emptied. Then a Chinese gentleman approached us to inquire whether we knew anything about the Bangladeshi delegation. We explained that we were it, so he escorted us to our chauffeur-driven car to start a most extraordinary tour. We were met in every city we visited with a personal guide and car, and (depending on the particular guide) we were able to visit places not usually frequented by foreigners: English Corner in Hangzhou where we discussed even politically sensitive subjects with students keen on learning the language; a day-care center at a textile factory where children learned to use chopsticks by plucking marbles out of a bowl of water; and an agrarian commune where we watched the World Cup soccer championship match in Mexico on the commune leader's TV. The China we saw on this visit, however, paled in contrast to the booming society we saw a decade later. Our next visit was during the final stage of my career when I started advising countries in transition from communism to capitalism.

CHAPTER X ∿
MISSIONARIES AND MARXISTS

*M*y first trip as an adviser to a marxist country was unexpected. In 1990 the United Nations invited me to present a paper at a conference in Mongolia, a country that had just emerged from being a Soviet satellite and buffer zone between Russia and China. My assignment was to discuss industrial policy in emerging nations struggling to replace a centrally planned economy with a market economy.

Faced with the choice of getting to Ulaan Baatar via Moscow or Beijing, I unfortunately chose the former. At this time a transit passenger at Moscow airport was given a good lesson about what to expect in a command and control economy when central authority collapses. Upon arrival I wandered through the empty, cavernous corridors looking for someone to ask about my checked baggage, only to be told eventually that I needed a Russian visa to go to the baggage department. I was not allowed to have lunch without an airline voucher, but I was again told that I couldn't go to the airline desk to ask for one without a visa. So I dined on a candy bar bought from a duty-free shop while looking forward to a decent meal in my first-class seat on Aeroflot. But when I finally boarded my night flight to Siberia, the crew crammed me into an economy seat so that they could stretch out in the forward cabin, explaining that they needed to sleep because they were poorly paid and had to work a second job during the day.

My baggage of course never did arrive at my destination, so I had to get along with the clothes on my back and with what I was able to scrounge in Ulaan Baatar. My search for clothes provided another lesson on what to expect in an emerging economy. There was almost nothing to buy in regular stores, and the so-called "dollar shops" didn't sell things like socks and underwear. So I had to continue my search in the black market with a Mongolian colleague who knew what back alley doors to knock on. Flashing dollar bills under the noses of secretive vendors worked wonders; I was able to acquire a minimum

The Mallon clan on the fortieth anniversary of our marriage, 1990

wardrobe in a single afternoon. This kind of market capitalism always prospers in a command and control economy.

Conference participants were lodged in the government guest house, located in a lovely park populated by deer as large as horses, some with antlers eight feet across. An added attraction was the pack of wolves that came down from the mountains in the evening and howled under our windows while we slept. The guest house and nearby city showed signs everywhere of the long Russian occupation: grandiose public buildings with Spartan amenities, rundown rows of apartment houses, a pall of coal smoke partly obscuring the sky by day, stingy street lighting creating deep gloom at night, statues of Lenin or war heroes in each square, and all signs, even in the local language, written in Cyrillic script (the local script had been banned by the Soviets).

The Mongolian economy had been almost completely dependent on Russian aid and trade before they were drastically cut back after the disintegration of the Soviet Union. Now the country was desperately trying to find new sources of foreign exchange while carrying out massive reforms, both political and economic. A recently elected president and parliament were struggling to reduce government spending and controls and to stimulate private initiative while still protecting those who relied on the old socialist safety net. This was to become a familiar struggle in those emerging countries attempting rapid reform. The short-term result was also to become familiar: young, better-educated city dwellers and well-connected bureaucrats were best able to take advantage of the reforms, whereas government and state enterprise employees, farm workers, and pensioners were often losers.

Shock therapy vs. more gradual reform thus became one of the main topics of discussion in the conference. Our Mongolian colleagues, especially the "young turks," were the strongest advocates of rapid reform, whereas most foreign participants were more cautious. We were concerned that rushing reforms without adequate institutional support might not be sustainable. The country did not yet have a competent central bank, national budget office, tax administration, legal system, or other institutions essential for managing a modern market economy. It was not even possible to open a personal checking account in a bank or sell a piece of real estate, and there were few trained business managers, accountants, or lawyers. If rapid reform did not benefit the majority of citizens in a reasonable period of time, a backlash of disgruntled voters could bring the whole reform process tumbling down.

After the conference I returned home via Moscow, this time with a Russian visa. So in the airport I was able to search for my lost luggage in the huge warehouse where such things were stored, without success. I was told, however, that my bags had been shipped back to Frankfurt, and indeed I found them there. But before proceeding to Frankfurt I took advantage of my Russian visa to explore Moscow. What a mixture of market-capitalist influence and emerging-economy austerity! The driver of my airport taxi was playing a guitar song in Russian-accented English twang on the radio, "I didn't know how many friends I had until I went to Leningrad"; and when I gave him a pack of American cigarettes as a tip, he almost fell to his knees in thanks.

In my hotel I was warned to be careful going out at night, and a security guard was stationed in front of the elevator on each floor. In the evening, the famous Arbat Street was nevertheless full of people watching the musicians, mimes, and portrait painters; listening to political debates; and sorting through the vast array of trinkets for sale (the hottest item seemed to be Gorby dolls). But there were lots of beggars too, and transactions in dollars had to be conducted se-

cretly. The biggest surprise, however, was hearing commercial adver-
tisements on Radio Moscow!

Eighteen months later I was invited back to Mongolia by the United
Nations, but this time I chose to go via Beijing. My luggage was not
lost, and I was permitted to occupy my business class seat on the flight
to Ulaan Baatar; but the aisles were so crowded with bundles that even
the attendants were unable to move around. Did this mean that the
Mongolian economy was now booming? Hardly – I soon found out
that most of the bundles contained contraband for the new elite who
paid poor customs officials to look the other way.

This was the first of three trips I made to Mongolia in 1992, all of
them having to do with planning technical assistance for the country. The situation reminded me of Bangladesh – foreign assistance
organizations and government agencies both were scrambling for a
piece of the action, each trying to establish influential relationships
and to promote their own interests. The Japanese wanted to develop
strong trading ties, the Germans were trying to take advantage of
former East German connections, Americans were promoting private
business interests, etc. The UNDP therefore adopted a strategy called
NaTCAP (national capacity building) intended to help the Mongolian government "articulate its own priorities and institute its own
procedures for managing technical assistance."

NaTCAP seemed to make a lot of sense under the circumstances,
but it soon became painfully clear that the Mongolian government
did not yet have the capacity to strengthen its capacity for managing
technical assistance. There was no one in the government who had
ever dealt with international aid donors except the Soviet Union,
which of course imposed its own priorities and procedures. Very few
officials could understand a foreign language except Russian, and no
one was even responsible for obtaining information on the technical
assistance currently being received, much less for coordinating it.
Worst of all, government officials had only the foggiest idea of what
was needed to manage a modern market economy.

I therefore decided to brush up the Russian I learned at Princeton
and to offer my services as a resident adviser to help the government
undertake this daunting institution and people-building task. So even
though I was preparing to retire from HIID by this time, Nacha and
I took off for Mongolia in late 1992 to explore possibilities. We were
received hospitably with a rare government car, driver, and English-
speaking guide. People were extremely friendly, even in the country-

side, where a nomad family received us in their *gher* with offerings of fermented mare's milk and a recently born lamb for Nacha to hold. Nacha was also offered the directorship of an international school that expatriate residents had started for their children.

We found that other aspects of living in Ulaan Baatar, however, would be depressing: living in a cramped, stuffy apartment; suffering periodic cutoffs of heating and hot water while the city-wide distribution system was being cleaned; eating cabbages and uncastrated mutton in the absence of other fresh produce; and experiencing those long, cold winters with nothing else to do but read books at night. It therefore came as a relief personally when the government and funding agency decided to continue relying on technical assistance from a group of young reformers, ironically led by a Harvard economist, Jeffrey Sachs, who soon afterward became the new director of HIID!

Had I stayed on as a resident adviser to the government, I would have witnessed the gradual polarization of Mongolian society into winners and losers. Many new hotels, nightclubs, restaurants, and stores were opened to cater to the well-to-do, while the ranks of the unemployed, homeless beggars, thieves, and prostitutes grew dramatically. Finally, in 1997, the reformist president was voted out of office and replaced by the leader of Mongolia's former hard-line communist party.

Later that same year I came out of retirement to accompany a HIID colleague on a mission to another former dependency of the Soviet Union, Kazakstan. The newly independent country had adopted rapid political and economic reforms similar to those in Mongolia with similar results. Pockets of luxury flourished amid widespread hardship, although the situation was less grim than in Mongolia. Kazakstan was a middle income country that had been the center of the Soviet ballistic missile program, so it had many well-trained workers as well as large, untapped petroleum reserves. Perhaps it will be able to survive economic polarization without the political backlash that occurred in Mongolia, although the experience of other rapid reformers has been very mixed.

Asian marxists, in contrast, adopted more gradual reforms, perhaps influenced by the successful dragons. South Korea, Taiwan, and Singapore had implemented export-led growth strategies without political liberalization by establishing close partnerships between business and the state. Vietnam and China wisely started by

decontrolling agricul-
ture, and then they pro-
moted export-oriented
businesses under differ-
ent forms of ownership
without destroying the
state sector or introduc-
ing sweeping economic
reforms. I was very interested to observe directly
what was going on, so in
1992 I readily accepted
an invitation to join a
World Bank team to con-
duct a couple of semi-
nars on the reform of
state-owned enterprises
in Vietnam.

One seminar was held
in Ho Chi Minh City (ex-
Saigon) and the other in

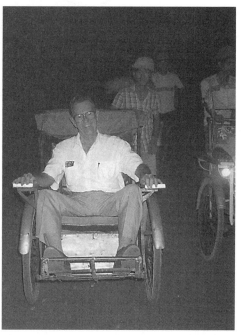

Sitting easy, Vietnam, 1992

Hanoi. What a contrast between two major cities in the same country! The former was bustling with activity: the streets were filled with
roaring motorcycles and bikes, imported goods were on sale everywhere, and only old people wore traditional dress. Hanoi, on the other
hand, seemed more like a sleepy provincial town: people got around
on bicycles and rickshaws, exercised in the park at dawn, and closed
up shop during the heat of the day, and there was only one first-class
hotel! It appeared that the government was allowing Ho Chi Minh
City to be a test case for reforms before allowing them to spread to
the rest of the country. Seminar participants here seemed especially
interested and alert, but we found it extremely difficult in both cities
to explain the concept of free-market competition.

Even our interpreters seemed unable to understand that government must allow unprofitable business firms to fail in a freely competitive market. Most social services – housing, health, child care, even
education – were provided by enterprises, in which workers considered that they had ownership rights. It was inconceivable that firms
upon which their livelihood depended could go belly-up and leave
them stranded! I doubt that we converted anyone in our audiences

Rickshaw no longer in service, China, 1995

to the competitive capitalist faith, but I gained a profound respect for the capacity of the Vietnamese people to adjust to change when given the opportunity.

Despite having suffered the ravages of a horrendous war, few signs of the suffering remained. Almost everything had been rebuilt except for the shattered forest on top of a warren of tunnels that had been dug to infiltrate Saigon during the conflict. The tunnels had been turned into a national monument so that tourists could appreciate how Vietcong soldiers survived underground despite repeated efforts to bomb, gas, or flood them out. Almost every family in Vietnam is reported to have a war cripple, but we saw few amputees or wheelchairs in the streets (we were told that most of them stay indoors because they are ashamed to be seen in public). But we did not feel any animosity directed toward us. Our good-natured hosts even took us on a day-long excursion to the beach where the government plans to develop a resort for surfers.

I was even more eager now to return to China, where gradualism had been enshrined as the official strategy of reform with the motto of "crossing the river by feeling for the stones." So in 1995 I accepted an invitation to go there on a lecture tour, again accompanied by Nacha as we had done almost ten years earlier. Beijing was unrecognizable! Tall buildings and shopping malls had sprung up everywhere; the streets were jammed with motor vehicles instead of cycles; and there was a McDonald's or Kentucky Fried Chicken on almost every other block. English was widely spoken, and my lecture audiences seemed especially interested in hearing how U.S. public enterprises are managed. So much change in so short a period of time, apparently without the stark contrast between winners and losers I had read about and seen in the former Soviet Union, could not possibly be typical outside of the capital and perhaps some special economic zones like Guangzhou, I thought. I was therefore very curious to continue my tour to other cities in China.

Our next stop was Dalian on the north coast. Upon arrival we were obliged to pull down our window shades in the plane so we could not see the large naval base there, but once in the city we could roam around freely. Another boom town! Placards were posted in prominent places proclaiming that Dalian would soon be the next Hong Kong. And at the Management Training Center of Dalian University of Science and Technology, I didn't even need an interpreter to speak to the crowd of bright young students, who demonstrated their command of English by even laughing at my jokes. The communist party official who chaired the meeting, however, must have thought that things were getting a little out of control, because during the discussion period he insisted that all questions from the audience be submitted to him in writing before I replied.

Old attitudes were even more evident in the next city on our tour. At first we were denied permission to visit Fuzhou further down the coast opposite Taiwan, perhaps because of military maneuvers being conducted off shore. The government relented at the last minute, and I was allowed to address the local System Reform Committee on restructuring state-owned enterprises. The senior committee members, who appeared to be fairly high-ranking party officials, insisted that local enterprises had already been restructured and didn't have any more problems. I could see flickers of skepticism on some younger faces in the back row, but despite my effort to draw them out, they preferred to remain silent. Our dinner host that night, the director of the Fujian Foreign Affairs Office, was on the other hand open and apologetic, explaining that it would take time to overcome the opposition of many older communist cadres to reform.

Our tour then continued inland after a brief stopover in the incredible boom town of Guangzhou. From what we could see in Chongqing and Xian, the interior of the country was also developing, although we heard a lot of complaints about inland China being left behind as a backwater. Unfortunately, I did not have an opportunity to enter into discussions with local officials and students about reforms in these two cities. In Chongqing I attended a large, formal conference with other speakers, and the visit to Xian was Nacha's idea. She wanted to see the fabulous terra-cotta soldiers and the old walled city that once was the eastern terminus of the legendary Silk Road.

What I had read and seen of open market reforms in marxist countries was sufficient, however, to raise serious questions in my mind about the capitalist missionary zeal of many of my economist colleagues. Judging by results, the more gradualist East Asian strategy of reform was a clear winner over the Western shock therapy approach. The East Asian dragons, Vietnam, and China had achieved rates of economic growth over a decade or more that had never been witnessed before in human history. In contrast, most marxist countries of Eastern Europe and the former Soviet Union, which attempted to introduce rapid economic and political liberalization simultaneously, had suffered severe economic recessions and high rates of inflation that imposed great hardship on the most vulnerable members of society.

Did this experience vindicate the superiority of gradual reform over shock therapy in emerging market economies, and perhaps in developing countries in general? I doubt it. Societies with strong capitalist traditions and institutions – like Chile, Czechoslovakia, and even the former South Vietnam – can be expected to adjust less painfully to shock therapy. Other societies, in which profound changes in institutions are needed to support policy reform, may be better off changing more gradually. For a foreign adviser like myself, I still thought that the basic question was, Is it proper for outside economists to try to dictate the pace of reform and type of regime that a sovereign nation should adopt? Answers to these questions have become clearer to me now that the current stage of world economic history and my own career seem to have come full circle.

CHAPTER XI ∽

COMING FULL CIRCLE

I am now finishing these memoirs in 1998, fifty years after I met Nacha and became interested in international development, and five years after my retirement from HIID. But suddenly I have the feeling that I am reliving a bit of the past. The awesome East Asian dragons and their clones (Indonesia, Malaysia, and Thailand) have been seriously wounded, calling into question their model of successful economic development. Even world market globalization itself, the Shangri-la of missionary technocrats, has been challenged because it fosters international financial instability and favors flighty capital at the expense of less mobile labor. And HIID is experiencing another crisis of confidence even more serious than that of the early 1970s. These and other recent events have given me the impression that the field of international development as well as my own professional life have come full circle.

Even our family seems to have completed a circuit. In 1997 we visited our daughter Florel and family in Chile, where she and her husband were bonding with Nacha's extended family and carrying out research on new books, while on sabbatical leave from their university. Our daughter Nanine was happily remarried and living not far from where I grew up in Southern California, where she works for a multinational firm. Three of our grandsons had learned Spanish, and the oldest of them was getting married and planning to spend his honeymoon in our winter retreat in Baja California. So this seems like a good time to reflect on the significance of events over the last fifty years, both for my own life and career as well as for the development advisory profession in general.

My professional circle began in the 1950s world of relatively high protective tariffs and foreign exchange controls, when most poor countries lacked both the institutions and the skills to manage economic policy well. My mission as a foreign adviser, financed mainly by the Ford Foundation, was to help build policy planning and analysis institutions and train people to run them. Then in the 1970s an

*First grandson Alan's wedding
with Melissa, June 1998*
below: Dennis and Nacha
right: Bob, Melissa, Alan, and Nanine
bottom: Nacha, Raffi, Raji, Florel,
Steve, and Dick

increasing number of countries began to open up their economies, influenced by the phenomenal success of the East Asian dragons and pressured by international financial agencies. Economic policy advisers, now financed mainly by these agencies, turned into activist missionaries preaching free-market reforms. By the 1990s a new group of clients appeared on the scene, former communist countries eager to be converted into capitalist dragons. But most of these countries resemble those poor nations of the 1950s that lacked the institutions and skills to manage a modern market economy; and the open mar-

Nanine with second husband, Bob, married March 1991

ket model they want to emulate now looks more risky than they first imagined.

Coming full circle does not of course mean that the advice we new missionaries have been giving is misdirected. The superior efficiency of market over command economies is indisputable. Experience over recent decades instead confirms what I said earlier about the extreme complexity of the reform *process*. Markets do not work efficiently unless they are supported by adequate institutions, and reforms are not sustainable in democratic societies if new rules of the game create more losers than winners. To complicate matters further, the world is becoming homogenized economically and technologically much faster than institutions and people. The balance of power is shifting away from local communities and sovereign nation-states, which long served as the main vehicles for forging social consensus among classes, generations, and interest groups. Power is now increasingly being wielded by an impersonal global market, in which only the fittest can expect to prosper.

In advanced countries like the United States, Japan, and those in Western Europe, global market pressures are manifested mainly in the struggle of private enterprises to cut costs by downsizing and outsourcing procurement to cheaper suppliers. In these countries the stress of adjustment has so far been felt primarily by displaced workers and the poorly educated. In less-developed countries and transitional economies, on the other hand, pressure has been exerted more on downsizing government by privatizing state-owned enterprises, eliminating controls and subsidies, and allowing markets to determine wages, prices, interest rates, and exchange rates. In these countries the impact of adjustment has fallen most heavily on a much broader spectrum of society – the typical businessman using outmoded technology with little capital; the many people without access to modern communications and transportation; those that depend on subsidized food, housing, and health services; old age pensioners; and redundant employees of government agencies and enterprises.

Rapid market reforms in less-developed countries and transitional economies are thus not likely to generate social consensus unless the shock of adjustment is cushioned and reform losers are given a fair chance to improve their lot in the foreseeable future. Unfortunately, markets in most of these countries are not very fair – they are often dominated by entrepreneurial elites with close political connections who take advantage of reforms to feather their own nests. Rapid reforms in these countries have therefore been accompanied too often by a rending of the social fabric, if not an outright breakdown in law and order. In Russia, Mongolia, and a number of other countries, citizens almost seem to be reliving the experience of the U.S. during the days of the Wild West, the business robber barons, or the famous gangsters of the 1930s. Why is this so? I believe it is because most former communist countries and many LDCs, especially in Africa, lack the institutional infrastructure necessary to civilize the new rules of the game.

In mature democratic societies this infrastructure consists of programs to help the less fit, such as unemployment insurance, social security, food stamps, and worker retraining programs that do not depend on direct government intervention in markets or on paternalistic employer-provided welfare. Equally important are effective judicial and legal systems to protect property and other individual rights, checks and balances on abuse of government power such as conflict of interest legislation and reliable public audits, credible government regulation of markets in which competition or public knowledge is limited, a really free investigative press, and a well-educated populace that understands how to make these institutions work properly.

So I think that the concerns I have expressed throughout these memoirs about the conduct of new missionaries are still valid. Economic policy advisers are on a sounder footing if they teach more than preach and are willing to consider gradual reforms when that approach is more in harmony with a country's stage of institutional development. This is especially true for the countries that are likely to request economic policy advice in the future, namely those in Africa and in transition from communist rule. Most other countries no longer want, and probably don't need, foreign technical assistance to strengthen national economic policy planning and analysis. By and large they now have a critical mass of Western-trained economists, and many Latin American and Asian countries have "graduated" to the rank of NICs, or newly industrialized countries. Countries recently liberated from colonialism or long communist rule, on the other hand, are still struggling to integrate diverse ethnic and religious groups or old regime supporters into modern, democratic nation-states. Judging from the decades-long struggle of Latin America after independence from Spain to consolidate warring fiefdoms and factions into viable nation-states, this process may take quite a long time.

In the meantime, leaders trying to consolidate political power and forge social consensus in nascent African nations often resort to the most blatant forms of cronyism, nepotism, and corruption. Africa is of course not unique in this respect; it happened in the urban melting pots of the United States during the period of massive immigration. I remember talking about this subject with Bolivian president Paz Estensoro not long after he led the 1952 revolution that toppled the tin barons and for the first time integrated the majority indigenous population into national life. Up to this time Indian communities had never participated in running the country; they were even forbidden by law to appear in prominent places in the capital city. So President Paz said that he made a conscious decision to give them a stake in the new regime by allowing them to rip off the government.

Widespread cronyism, nepotism, and corruption may be an effective means for building allegiance and consolidating political power in fragmented societies trying to become politically viable nation-states, but such an environment is not conducive to the establishment of healthy, competitive market economies. Without transparent, impersonal, and well-enforced rules of the game, the battle for competitive advantage can turn into a struggle for survival in a political jungle, in which only privileged insiders have a fair chance of success. This situation appears to exist not only in emerging market economies but also in most of East Asia.

In the last chapter I observed that the East Asian model of more gradual reform – "crossing the river by feeling for the stones" – seemed to have been more successful than the shock therapy strategies adopted by many LDCs and the former Soviet bloc. Instead of rapidly eliminating safety nets provided by state-owned enterprises and dismantling command and control regimes, East Asian countries have promoted development of parallel free market systems. These systems have been so successful in promoting rapid economic growth that opposition from reform losers did not materialize. But now that the

East Asian dragons themselves are faced with a dose of shock therapy and economic recession to overcome the current financial crisis, a rising number of losers are beginning to revolt. What went wrong?

The cronyism, nepotism, and corruption that are prevalent in many LDCs and in command and control societies tend to undermine one of the basic institutional supports of free markets in a globalized economy – the effective government regulation of financial markets. If regulations are lax and depositors and investors lose confidence in the soundness of local financial institutions, a panic flight of capital is inevitable. Globalization therefore turns out to be a two-edged sword: closely allied entrepreneurs and politicians have shown they can take good advantage of globalized trade, but globalized money can bring them down if they use insider influence to milk financial institutions. Mobile money thus acts like a sword of Damocles to help keep governments honest in open economies, but there is also a downside. Money is very nervous: it can go racing in and out of countries propelled by fear and rumors, even destabilizing economies that are fundamentally sound.

We have therefore entered a new world in which almost no nation is safe from the devastating effects of international capital surges, especially a country threatened by economic crisis. Such a country appears to be faced with an unsavory choice, reimpose government controls or undergo shock therapy, unless the crisis is already so severe that controls would be ineffective. Bolivia in the mid-1980s is a good example. The country was suffering another devastating hyperinflation like the one I witnessed in the 1950s, when I had to pay for a haircut with a check because it was too awkward to carry enough bank notes to pay for it in cash. A popular joke at the time was that thieves who stole an armored bank truck dumped the worthless currency it contained in the street so that they could get away with the truck more quickly. Under these chaotic conditions, shock therapy that re-establishes some order by freeing the exchange rate and forbidding the government from printing more money can even reverse the deterioration of social consensus, despite rising unemployment and economic recession.

Interestingly enough, the foreign adviser responsible for persuading the Bolivian government to adopt this strategy of reform was none other than Jeffrey Sachs, a "conquistador," like Raul Prebisch or Richard Gilbert, who was at the time of this writing the director of HIID. After Bolivia he moved on to persuade governments of former Soviet bloc countries to follow similar strategies that not only decontrol markets but call for the massive privatization of state-owned enterprises. Supporting institutional infrastructure in most of these countries, however, is unfortunately a good deal more wobbly than it was even in Bolivia. In Russia rapid privatization of SOEs therefore allowed political insiders to gain control of valuable business assets; the old state safety net was shredded before alternative welfare programs could be introduced and properly financed; and many less advantaged members of society have been unable to take advantage of the new opportunities provided by the lifting of controls. Under these appalling circumstances it would take a prophet to lead people to the promised land. My advice is, let local leaders play prophet; new missionaries should not be driven by the prophet motive.

HIID's experience in Russia also provides another lesson about the dangers faced by activist new missionaries in politically turbulent countries. The institute has strict guidelines for avoiding adviser conflicts of interest, but they did not dissuade the University from ordering a complete review of the organization and management of HIID when a conflict of interest case arose recently. The case involved advisers helping to develop securities markets in Russia who became engaged in questionable dealings while working in an agency embroiled in a high-profile struggle between local political rivals. A lower profile might have helped keep the advisers out of trouble or at least facilitated a more discreet resolution of the matter. But the University is now insisting on stricter monitoring of HIID's overseas operations, a job that I'm afraid neither academics nor university administrators are well suited for.

At the same time the University again raised the unresolved issue of HIID's contribution to research at Harvard. The institute has responded by trying to internalize the culture clash I mentioned in Chapter III. HIID research and most of its teaching will be merged with those of the Kennedy School of Government, while foreign advisory work will be managed separately. Will the institute be able in this way to reconcile internally the clash between the cultures of two very different lines of business any better than was done before? If the answer is negative, HIID will almost inevitably lose its ability to offer a unique career path to professionals like me who want to combine resident advisory work overseas with a scholarly life back home. We would be obliged to select between two separate career paths, a choice that would make more lucrative jobs in international and private consulting organizations increasingly attractive.

HIID thus seems to be evolving into an organization quite different from the one I originally joined. The DAS consisted of a relatively small group of economists committed to spending half their time in residence overseas helping to build institutions and provide in-service training for government technocrats. The new HIID is taking shape as a multidisciplinary, university teaching and research institute that is committed to advancing the frontier of knowledge in the field of development. Future foreign advisory work will likely consist mainly of helping to disseminate research results to already established institutions abroad, including an increasing number of regional and international organizations. This trend is already apparent in the fields of environmental protection, public health, and – especially under Sachs' leadership – in macroeconomic policy, in which HIID is even becoming involved in redesigning the architecture of international aid and finance.

The new HIID that is emerging strikes me as being more in tune with Harvard's scholarly self-image and modus operandi than the old organization was. But it is not yet clear how career foreign advisers who remain with the institute will fit into the scheme of things, except when they are on assignment abroad. In addition to generating project overhead income to finance HIID's administrative costs, they can also help build bridges linking Harvard research with practical applications to problem solving in client countries. Resident advisers are in a much better position than short-term academic consultants to learn about how things really work in the countries they advise, and to bond with, and win the confidence of, local counterparts. Experienced overseas advisers also should be able to give economic policy advice the nuance it needs to make it consistent with a country's level of institutional development.

I think my own experience is still instructive in these regards. In Bangladesh I tried to help our counterparts identify windows of opportunity for playing positive-sum games, that is, reforms that create mostly winners. I have also found many such opportunities in other countries where I've worked. Conversely, we could also help our counterparts spot losers in zero-sum reform games, in which winners benefit mainly at the expense of losers. We could then help counterparts design measures to ease the transitional pain of losers or to redistribute the benefits of reform. The posture I envisage for foreign advisers is similar to the one I assumed in Colombia, where I tried to maintain a low profile so as to oblige counterparts to accept full responsi-

Almost half a century later on the terrace of the hotel where Nacha and Dick spent their honeymoon, Vina del Mar, Chile, 1997

bility for policy-reform recommendations. This posture helps not only to reinforce a sense of local ownership of the reform process but also to avoid the impression that governments that accept HIID's advice also receive Harvard University's seal of approval. The Harvard community would not be happy if this impression, regardless of its validity, circulated widely.

I therefore still think that career foreign advisers have an important role to play in the new HIID, despite the lesser emphasis likely to be given to institution building and in-service training. But the bridges resident advisers help build between the university and the field to facilitate dissemination of research results must be able to carry two-way traffic. Overseas advisers who do not participate actively in HIID's research and teaching when back in Cambridge will not have sufficient knowledge to be effective disseminators. Arrangements for ensuring that this kind of synergy indeed takes place still remain to be worked out by the new HIID leadership.

Coming full circle in professional life thus raises intriguing and challenging questions. What will happen next? The only thing one can be pretty sure about is that the circle will not repeat itself. Some countries may throw out the new missionaries and try to close their economies again; but I am inclined to think that globalization will continue to offer such irresistible opportunities that most reforming countries will stay the course, perhaps by "feeling more for the stones."

As they try to strengthen institutional infrastructure to mitigate the risks of instability and unequal income redistribution caused by unfettered globalization, they will probably call on newer missionaries to help out. As we are discovering, globalized capitalism is arguably as difficult to manage for emerging nations today as a market economy was for poor LDCs in earlier days. The new HIID needs to be well positioned to meet this new challenge.

Finally, coming full circle in personal life has been a source of deep satisfaction for Nacha and me. The difficulties we have had to resolve together have firmly cemented our relationship. Our long journey without a destination seems to have helped many people we have worked with, and our daughters appear to have had rewarding experiences to justify the sacrifices they have had to bear. I hope that the next generations coming up, for whom these memoirs have mainly been written, will also find these memoirs instructive for sharpening their understanding of some of the challenges of the fast-changing world in which they live.

What I would most like our grandsons to gain from reading my story is a better understanding of what Nacha and I did with our lives and a deeper appreciation of the vast diversity of human societies around the world. To the extent they appreciate this diversity, they will be less inclined to pass judgment on how other people should behave. I also hope that they might gain some insights on how to handle life's inevitable disappointments, not as defeats but as challenges to overcome their own shortcomings and to adjust to an ever-changing world.

As for my younger professional colleagues, I hope that reading my memoirs will help them understand how much our profession has changed over the last half-century. Above all, I would like them to realize that there is no common formula for solving a country's problems. Each society must come up with its own formula, in which economic policy is only one important variable in a complex equation. We new missionaries can best help our counterparts carry out this daunting task by teaching more than preaching and by insisting that they themselves take full responsibility for their recommendations and actions. We must convince them that we are on their side, not agents of foreign organizations trying to enforce outside prescriptions for reform. The new missionary profession will remain a noble one so long as we resist the temptation to become crusaders.

Epilogue

$\mathcal{A}$ s might have been expected when HIID research and most of its teaching was transferred to the Kennedy School of Government, the University decided at the beginning of the year 2000 to dissolve the institute itself. The remaining pieces are being dispersed among Harvard professional schools that may be interested in picking them up. The unique experiment begun by Ed Mason thus comes to an end – no longer is the University likely to be able to offer a career path to scholarly development advisers who want to split their time between residence abroad and teaching and research at Harvard. The professional schools that pick up the pieces will offer career opportunities that conform to their own, mainly academic, criteria.

Not only has my own profession come full circle, but the rush toward world economic globalization also shows signs of slowing down, if not turning back. Interest groups fearing its negative consequences are mobilizing in opposition, as evidenced at the World Trade Organization conference in Seattle last year. International rules of the game that would strengthen protection of human rights, labor, and the environment are opposed by most less-advanced countries, which instead advocate changes in international financial arrangements and trade practices that more-advanced countries find difficult to stomach. To resolve these differences, less-developed countries will have to strengthen their regulatory and other institutions to compete successfully in open markets. Perhaps the sermon that many new missionaries have been preaching will therefore have to be revised to place more emphasis again on training and institution building.

In contrast, my personal life exemplifies continuity rather than coming full circle. Nacha and I will be celebrating our golden wedding anniversary in the year 2000. We plan to distribute both her mem-oirs and mine at a ceremony to renew our vows in the presence of our extended family and a few close friends. This is the way it should be – the cycle of life may come full circle in the wider world, but the personal relationships that bind people together should endure.